MATTERS OF
Life

WITH 10 KEYS TO HELP MAKE
YOUR LIFE MATTER

FRAN NGUYEN

FOREWORD

This book will take you on a heartfelt journey of love and purpose that will leave you encouraged, inspired and uplifted. Fran Nguyen has done a masterful job, weaving an intriguing tale set in a small biblical village with life giving principals. As the story unfolds, you will begin to feel what life would have been in a time where work was hard, life was simple yet challenging, and the future uncertain. Quite a contrast to our modern time, but with a message that is as relevant today as it was then. Among the key ingredients missing in our modern sophisticated societies are purpose and simplicity. Many people, both young and old, are void of a powerful sense of identity and quiet confidence to face the future. We are living in a time when the western world is the wealthiest it has ever been. Our modern technologies put computer processing power in everyone's pocket, medicinal advancements mean we are living longer, and we can access information and convenience unlike any time in history. However, with these advancements, the sad reality is that humanity is the most depressed, discouraged and discontent it has ever been. I believe the author touches on the answer to this modern-day epidemic in *Matters of Life*. This book provides 'success keys' for a life full of purpose and meaning in a simple and uncomplicated way. My hope is that you will enjoy its pages, absorb its truth, apply its wisdom, and discover with greater clarity your God-given purpose.

Andrew Zimmerman

Principal Business Advisor with Living Strategies Accounting and Tax
Apostolic Leader at Rivers Apostolic Centre

Acknowledgements

I would like to thank:

My God: for being there for me through thick and thin. No matter the difficulties or the issues that I have faced, I know that I can always count on Him. His promises are true every day!

My parents: for their support for all the things I have undertaken over the years, including going overseas, and then living in Australia. They gave me so much love and understanding. They never held me back from the projects that I undertook, which has enabled me to be an extraordinary person. I have lived in some of the weirdest places, and they have stood by me through it all!

My very dear friends, Rachel and Caesar Ferguson-Gow: for all their love and support and for putting up with me breezing in with yet another idea! Also for the many hours of discussion and the many meals we have shared. Love you both so much.

Jackie Pullinger: for offering me the opportunity to work in Hong Kong for a second innings, and for all her inspiration and passion. It was so good to witness the transformation of the Pillar Point Refugee Camp, and to see so many make positive changes to their lives.

I would also like to give huge thanks to my brother Martin Wells and his wife Gaynor for all their support and encouragement over the years, and for their belief in me that I could write a book, and then for their help in proofreading and critiquing the text. They undertook the tricky task and have been wonderful in their input and advice. I love and appreciate them enormously.

To Georgia Kirke at Write Buiness Results for helping me get my book into format and become a reality!

To all at JT FOXX Family First, and Andy Harringtons' JetSet-Speakers organisations, a big thank you for inspiration and training; without which I would not have dared to take the plunge. Thank you!

I would also like to thank all those at Vietnam Grace Church, Brisbane for their ongoing support and love. You are a real church family. Love you all.

There are too many other folk that I would like to thank, so to you all a Big Thank You.

CONTENTS

INTRODUCTION

Throughout my life, I have seen many babies born, and witnessed many people die, both physically and spiritually. Personally I am a daughter, a mother, a grandmother, an ex-wife, a sister, a friend, and now an author. I have travelled to over 40 countries. I have worked as a Registered Nurse in England, Pakistan, in the Vietnamese Refugee Camps in Hong Kong, and in Australia. In Hong Kong I worked with Jackie Pullinger and St. Stephen's society, where we helped heroin addicts come off drugs: cold turkey; through prayer. I have also worked as a Clinical Nurse, a Counsellor, as a Nurse with a Naltrexone Programme in a rapid detox setting, a Case Manager for Transformations Drug Rehabilitation House, and a Youth Coordinator for Vietnam Grace Church in Brisbane.

Besides all that, I have lived with a husband suffering from Post Traumatic Stress Disorder. This made life difficult not only for him, but also for myself, and our children. It was all the more difficult as culturally it was frowned upon to talk about family circumstances to outsiders. Finally, I was encouraged to make changes and so we are now moving on with our lives.

My boys and I are still dealing with the subsequent healing process. We push on to gain positive outcomes in our individual lives, knowing that we have all been through so much. We need the love and support of each other. It is never easy, as we have had to go through grief and loss without really understanding the reasoning behind it all. Yet we progress from day to day.

I hope that through reading this story: based on five verses in Luke 7:11-15; with the keys to life embedded in it, you too will be encouraged to step out and be bold enough to receive your own abundant life. Life is too short to wait for changes to happen, you have to make the effort to decide, and then act on them yourself.

I wish you all every success. Be bold. Be strong. Be courageous.

CHAPTER 1

"When you have the courage to become all of who you can be, your self-belief gives you the confidence to shine and inspire others."

Annie Lionnet

Zillah smiled with delight as she sat admiring her newborn son, as he cooed at her from his wooden cradle. Her husband, Caleb, stood with a huge smile on his face, as he too admired his newborn son. What a treasure the Good Lord had blessed him with: this tiny miracle. Zillah pondered in her heart: "What would their lives become now that they were three?"

The midwife had left early that morning, and they had had some moments to gather themselves together, whilst Caleb's mother had been in to prepare a stew for them.

Zillah looked around at their tiny dwelling made of rough hewn stone, with water pots standing in the shade by the door. Outside it was a blazing hot day, and the heat shimmered off the dusty road, which wound its way between the hamlets towards Capernaum. Her husband was a good man and had provided for their small family well; whitewashing the walls and ensuring that the inside of the dwelling was clean and dry. He kept a small herd of goats nearby, and they were able to make ends meet by selling the milk and cheeses that Zillah made, which supplemented the income that Caleb brought in from weaving.

Caleb was a well-respected man in their small town, and he took his place at the town gates with the other elders of their community. He was a leader among men. Not only was he a good merchant of goat products, but he was also a weaver of excellent cloth from both goat's hair and sheep's wool. The goat's cloth was used for outer garments and tent making. He was new to weaving woollen products and was looking to develop his flocks and add some sheep to his livestock. He worked hard at his loom. Zillah, his wife of three years, was a great support as she not only made the cheeses, but also helped with the preparation of the goat's hair, dyeing the cloth and the goatskins. As a family they were doing well, and now Caleb had an heir to carry on his name. He was very content with his life, though he had one major problem: a while back he had fallen and damaged his right leg, and now it was not straight and in wet weather it ached painfully.

Zillah stood and stretched, and headed outside to the lean-to kitchen, to the pots hanging over the fire. She stirred the goat stew they were having for their dinner, and threw in some carrots that had been grown by her neighbour and given as a gift after she'd delivered her baby. She returned to the main room of the house and was delighted to see her sister Miriam entering the house. She ran over to the crib, "Oh, look at him, he is adorable," she exclaimed. She bent over and scooped the baby up, turned to Caleb and said: "Well, then, what's his name?"

Caleb bent down and placed a kiss on his infant's head and said, "We've decided to call him Joshua, after his late uncle. It is a good strong family name." He smiled at Miriam, and ducked out of the doorway to go and check on the goat keeper he had hired to look after the goats during this auspicious time. Giving the sisters time together to cherish the baby. Women's talk!

Miriam exclaimed: "Oh, Zillah, he is so cute. I can't wait for my baby to come; it's only four more months. We are so blessed to have such hard-working husbands, and to be able to have children together. They can grow up and learn together, and get into mischief together!"

Zillah looked over to her younger sister and smiled, "Yes, Miriam, we are indeed blessed. We are to have our children growing up together. Plus it looks like the goats and the weavings are going well, so we will be well established in the community. Already the leaders are looking to Caleb to be the next Chief merchant in the town. We need the caravans to come through on their annual trek to buy our products. As you know, we are managing to increase our stock in readiness for their arrival. It will be a good year!"

Miriam looked down and was a bit sad as she said reflectively, "Yes, for you both. I just hope that Boaz will be able to work a little smarter, so that we have enough for our family. He has been struggling with the tax collectors a bit; they are really pushing him with paying up from last year. It has not been easy for us. The Romans have been making it a lot harder for carpenters these days. In fact that awful centurion, Brutus, and his mob, were out on the roads and Stefan was murdered over in Magdala last month, as there was a dispute about the taxes again!"

"Well I will get Caleb to have a chat with Boaz, maybe he could come in alongside us and we could increase the goat herd, and expand our family business a bit. Caleb really wants to concentrate on the weaving side a bit more, as he finds it difficult with his bad leg which has not mended so well after his fall a couple of years ago. He has discovered that going out into the hills is becoming more stressful, he is not walking as well as he would like."

"Oh, Zillah, that would be so wonderful! Do you think Caleb would really take him on? That would help our situation so much. Especially with our baby coming soon, that would be fantastic! It would also be a relief to have Boaz closer to hand, as he would not have to travel so far to other villages for work, then he would not be exposed to the Romans so much. Though on second thoughts, that might be harder as well, as he can be quite selfish, and wants things done yesterday, without any consideration to others' needs. I wish he understood me more! He does shout and is so demanding at times."

At that moment, little Joshua began to wriggle and squirm in his aunt's arms so Zillah took him from her sister. "Well young man," she said looking down at her son, "are you getting hungry then?" She carried him over to the rocking chair set in the corner, settled into it and began to feed her new charge. Soon, contented sounds were issuing from the corner. Zillah sat back in the rocking chair and smiled at her son. Miriam observed all that was happening and then sat at her sister's feet. "You look so happy," she said. Zillah looked fondly at her younger sister,. "Yes, I am very happy. It is so good to have a baby at last. We have had to wait for these three years, and now things are beginning to look so promising."

"Please could you help us? I find Boaz very difficult and it is not always so easy. I do try, but sometimes he just gets angry with me for no apparent reason. He is so impatient!" "Dearest Miriam, you will have to see what you can do to serve him better, and I will have a chat with Caleb to see if he can give him some guidance as to how to be a better husband. But you can't change him, though. He has to want to change himself, you have to work on yourself first!" The sisters smiled at each other and watched as the new baby slept peacefully in his mother's arms.

CHAPTER 2

> *"The real opportunity for success lies within the person and not in the job"*
>
> Zig Ziglar

Boaz was a strong young man, with large capable hands, which were wonderful at carpentry. He could turn his hand to make almost anything he was asked, from cartwheels, to rocking chairs, he was an expert craftsman. Yet, he was hot-headed and did not always think before opening his mouth, and he'd had a couple of close run-ins with the local legionnaires because of his quick tongue. He hated rules and regulations, and was quick to take offense at the way the country was being overrun by the soldiers, who seemed at times to take the law into their own hands. On the other hand, he was great fun to be with, definitely one of the boys! And if someone wanted assistance, Boaz was often the first person they called upon.

He was always ready to help out if someone was in need; he had a good heart and was as strong as an ox! It was just his fiery temper that got the better of him at times.

The day his baby was born he paced the floor of his brother-in-law's house, anxiously looking at Caleb, "What can I do, it's been hours now! I'm really worried this midwife doesn't know what she's doing, Miriam needs to hurry it up, it's taking too long!"

Caleb looked at Boaz understandingly. "You can't hurry these things, they will come when they're good and ready. Relax, Shauna knows what she's doing, she's been a midwife for twenty years. I think she's well practised by now! Be patient."
"Oh it's alright for you! Your son is doing well and is already four months old! And Zillah is amazing, she's learning to weave along with you, and managing to care for her son, the home and you!"

"Yes, she's a wonderful companion. We work well as a team, and she's a quick learner! I think the important thing is that we value each other and are best friends as well. I really honour her as a companion and encourage her in all that she does for us as a family. Perhaps you could give Miriam some more support, she has not had such a good pregnancy and it has been difficult for her in this heat!"

"Yeah, the weather has been stinking hot! Thank goodness you took me on as a herdsman with your flocks, it has saved me going into Capernaum where it has not only been hot, but the zealots have been active and causing disruption in the villages! I am well out of it, but it hasn't been easy in our house.

What with Miriam having difficulties with her pregnancy and being so short-tempered herself, she has not helped the situation. At least I can get out into the fields and be with the other herdsmen. It's quiet out there and we can have fun keeping the flocks safe. There will be a new batch of kids due soon, at least twenty goats are pregnant, which will be excellent timing for the upcoming festive season."

"More to the point, you are about to be a father, and you will need to be around to support your wife and child. You may have to take on some local carpentry jobs. I know that you could work here in town. You are a skilled craftsman and you could get work around here instead of having to travel to the other villages and towns. Miriam could do with you at home a bit more. She adores you, you know, but she has been getting so tired in this last month. She could do with some of your love and encouragement. She is your treasure you know! Be at home a bit more. At least until she has learnt how to care for your newest family member!"

Just then little Sarah, Shauna's daughter, who had been running errands to support her mother, was commandeered to be a messenger and was sent to the house to get Boaz: "Shaun said you can come now. The baby has arrived!"

"What! Finally! Come on Caleb let's go and meet my offspring!"
"No," said Caleb, "You go. This is an important family time. You and Miriam must savour this moment. Besides, your mother is there, and she will want to rejoice with you at the arrival of her first grandchild! I'll come round later. Peace be with you."

Boaz rushed out of the door, and dashed down the street to his house, which was only a couple of streets away. The streets were only narrow, just wide enough to fit a heavily laden donkey, and so Boaz brushed past his neighbours, who all cheered him on, knowing full well what he was in such a hurry for!

Boaz flung the door of his house open and saw the gathering around Miriam, who had his mother, Debra, Shauna the midwife and Zillah in attendance. The house felt pretty crowded. From the depths of the room, a small tired voice spoke up, "Hello Boaz dear, look we have a gorgeous daughter, she is so adorable!"

The girls parted so that Boaz could see on the bed his exhausted, but thrilled wife holding out to him a small bundle. Boaz hesitated, so Zillah took the child and passed her into Boaz's waiting arms. At first he held her awkwardly but then he drew her into his embrace. As he cradled her, she looked up into her father's eyes. "Oh, she is so precious, and so tiny," he breathed. He gently rocked her in his arms and moved to the chair in the corner. He sat down and the two just gazed into each other's eyes for about ten minutes! Miracles were happening before their eyes as they watched this big man just melt at the sight of his baby girl. Many thoughts were going through his mind as he gradually took on board the new responsibilities he now had. To be a father to such a tiny person, his daughter! She looked so perfect, he felt his heart swell with pride and love for this, his beautiful child. He looked lovingly over to Miriam, "Sweetheart, I think we should call her Naomi, after my aunt. She was a strong woman and our daughter will also be an ambitious woman with an amazing destiny to fulfil! He smiled more lovingly at her than Miriam had ever remembered, and her heart swelled with warmth and delight. Everything is going to be all right after all she thought.

Shauna, Debra and Zillah finished tidying up bid the little family good bye, and left Boaz with his girls.

CHAPTER 3

"Courage is the first of human qualities because it is the quality which guarantees all others."

Winston Churchill

Brutus was cleaning his broadsword, as he gathered his men to make another sortie into the villages. They were escorting Matthew to round up unpaid taxes so that Festus, the governor, could pay for the next games due in two months time, to celebrate the arrival of important dignitaries who were coming from Rome to view the region. They were in the seaside town of Jaffa, and had been commissioned to collect taxes in and around Jericho for the next few weeks.

A boy, one of the many street urchins who hung around the Roman soldiers so that they could earn a piece of bread, and sometimes gain attention, brought round his horse. Brutus quickly mounted and rallied his men, "Come on men, let's get this show on the road. I fancy some roasted goat tonight, what do you say?" Max, his second in command also mounted his horse, and laughed with the men, "Yeah, and a good place to lay our heads tonight! Emmaus and Jericho here we come!" Just then Matthew appeared, carrying his tablets and stylus to document all the takings. "Get him his donkey, boy!" roared Brutus. The small boy dressed in scruffy rags, dashed off to do his bidding. He appeared minutes later leading a small donkey, with a blanket on its back. He gave Matthew a leg up, and held the reins until Matthew was settled with all his bits and pieces around him. The Tax Collector was nervous and anxious, he hated going on these trips. He was despised by the men he worked for; and hated by the people he had to squeeze taxes from, he felt miserable and helpless for he could see no way out of his current situation. He was as much a prisoner of his circumstances as the rest of them. The only reason he was given the privilege of riding on the donkey was that his short little legs could not keep up with the fast pace set by the soldiers, and he would have tired too easily and been more of a burden on the men. Max took up the reins of his horse and those of the donkey, and guided them both to the rear of the group.

The troop of twenty soldiers assembled in formation and Brutus rode out ahead of them, with Max and Matthew following on behind. As they passed through the city gates, a few local men were standing there. Noticing the tax gatherer they spat towards Matthew and looked at him bitterly, "Tax collector!" they said derogatorily. Max hastily pulled on the reins and guided his horse and the donkey into a trot, making the men step out of the way. "Leave him alone, he is about Rome's business", he said sternly. They trotted off up the road after the soldiers without further ado.

The road was dusty and the day was already hot, as the sun beat down on the small group making its way towards Emmaus and on to Jericho and the outlying villages. These were the areas from which they would be collecting taxes from the local populace.

Brutus was in a good mood; he loved being in command, and had a good bunch of men with him. He was a veteran of many battles, and had captured several slaves for the arena. One of his captives had made a name for himself in the games at Caesarea and would be fighting the huge African slave Titan, who was becoming well known in the Roman arena. The festival being arranged was to be a grand affair, and so Titan and other gladiators were being shipped over with other dignitaries from Rome. All the soldiers were looking forward to the festival and the potential promises of being posted back to Rome one day! They marched solidly for five hours and then Max called for a break in the shade of some olive trees in a grove nearby. They all headed for the scanty shade and water was distributed to everyone. "OK, listen up. We will have an hour's break now, rest, have something to eat and we will resume our journey and aim to be at Emmaus, our half way point, by night fall."

They all settled down for a much-needed rest. Matthew was not used to riding such long distances and could feel his muscles aching already; it was going to be a long trip! He groaned inwardly and tried to catch some sleep in the shade of the olive tree he had found to sit under by himself. He observed his fellow travellers; they were already lying in the shade, eyes shut, napping whilst they could, while Max kept a lookout on the knoll above the grove. The two horses were tethered nearby with the donkey, and all were grabbing the opportunity to be busily munching on whatever they could find in the sparse grasses around. Matthew lay back and looked up through the leaves at the blue sky and thought about the weird situation he found himself in.

"Oi, you, up you get, we're back on the road!'

Startled, Matthew roused himself. He must have drifted off! He clambered up and over to the donkey, he had difficulty getting on its back and the soldiers jeered at him, "Look at the dog, he can't even get on a donkey by himself!" Someone gave him a leg up and he sat shame faced, and furious at the same time. "Get a move on there money bags, we need to get to our next camp in Emmaus before sundown," Brutus shouted at him from the back of his horse, and turned and headed out to the road. The others all laughed at Matthew, and quickly marched out after their leader back onto the road. Brutus was impatient to get to Emmaus, as he wanted to meet up with an old friend who had been posted there. Eagerly anticipating the spit roast that had been promised he set a fast pace and all the men marched in formation behind him, with Matthew and Max again bringing up the rear. Matthew already bouncing up and down uncomfortably on the back of the little donkey.

CHAPTER 4

"Just know, when you truly want success, you'll never give up on it. No matter how bad the situation may get."

Unknown

"There it is!" Brutus pointed ahead as they climbed the small hill, where they could see, in the distance, a collection of palm trees and the stone walls of the Emmaus township. "I'll go ahead and meet up with my friend, Max you carry on, I'll come out and meet you when I have located him." He spurred his horse and cantered off in the town's direction.

The rest of the group picked up their pace, galvanised by the thought of rest and good food, and headed towards the township with renewed vigour. Max took over command, handed the donkey's reins to the nearest foot soldier and trotted to the head of the group. "Come on you men," He encouraged. "We will be having roast goat tonight! Step up your pace and we will be in the shade with full bellies in no time!" A cheer rose up from twenty hungry and thirsty throats. They all pressed on up the road, close on Brutus' heels, eager to get to their destination for the night.

Finally arriving at the gates to the town, they were met by Brutus with a wry smile. "Come on you lot! Follow me." He led them round the walls of the town to a large villa just inside the rear gate. They went through the entrance, and turned into a small alley, which opened out into a large courtyard. "Here, this is my friend Maximillian's place. We can bed down the animals in the stable over there, and you can all rest in these rooms off the courtyard. You, Taxman, can sleep in the hay barn with the animals. Come, Max. Let me introduce you to our host."

Max turned to follow Brutus, and then turned back and spoke to the leader of the foot soldiers: "Julius, take care of the Taxman, keep an eye on him. Assign someone to care for the animals, and I'll be back shortly to make sure you all get food and have a place to sleep." With that he turned and went with Brutus to find Maximillian. They headed into a cool atrium where Maximillian and his wife, Julia, were reclining at a table, drinking wine from silver goblets. "Come and join us friends," he called and sat up on his couch, "there are places here for you, but first go and wash the dust off your feet and get comfortable, and then we can dine. You must be hungry and thirsty after your journey!" He called over a servant who was waiting in the shadows, and indicated that he should take the two men to freshen up.

Shortly after, Brutus and Max re-entered the atrium and lay on the couches next to their hosts, each was given a goblet of wine. "Welcome to my house!" Said Maximillian jovially. We have managed to procure two goats which are now on the spits out the back, and will be ready shortly for us and your men to enjoy a good meal!" He smiled at the two Roman soldiers and then nudged Brutus. "Hey, and I got a dancing girl and some minstrels to come and do their thing for your entertainment tonight!" He grinned at his friend and started to talk about the difficulties of keeping the peace in this troubled region. Max took a look around the room, and then leaned towards his host and said: "Thank you so much for putting up with us all tonight, it is much appreciated. The men are pleased to have a break from the journey, and we are grateful for this opportunity to rest safely for the night." He smiled at Maximillian and his wife.

Julia laughed, "It is nice to have some diversion in this dreadful place in the middle of nowhere. It has been an age since we last had such a number of guests! It gives us a chance to have some decent conversation, to catch up on the latest news, and for Maximillian to entertain again. So thank you for coming!" "It's a needs must journey, as we have to get some money for Festus to host these games coming up! We've got this little taxman with us; he will be grubbing for the money. The region around Jericho is overdue to pay their taxes, so we may have some local issues to sort out! But the games will be something to look forward to! It will be a pretty big affair, and I know that the men are getting excited about it all. Will you be coming over to Caesarea to watch?"

"Oh yes!" she responded, "My sister and her husband are also coming over with the delegation from Rome, and so we will most definitely be there, I can't wait! I haven't seen Flavia for ages! She has now got two children and they will be coming over as well. It will be so exciting to have time together, and to meet her son and daughter. Although I am somewhat surprised that they are coming, due to the situation out here! Of course they will be bringing some of their servants with them as well, so we will have a house full at the time! But Maxi here has managed to arrange a villa for us right by the sea, not far from the arena, so we will have some excellent entertainment, and opportunities to meet others who are coming for the occasion!" "You're fortunate to have a family gathering. But now, please excuse me, I must go and see to the men. Are they to have a goat for their meal?"

Maximillian turned from chatting to Brutus and said: "Yes Max, that's right. They are to have one of the goats for themselves, and to enjoy a good meal. I have also procured some mead for them. That should put them in a good mood!" He laughed, "Nothing like a good mead to ease travel weariness, and worries about back home! Don't worry my friends, I haven't forgotten you either, we will have a great evening together. Max, you go see to your men, and when you come back, we will begin our evening!" He winked at Brutus, and they rose and left the atrium together.

Max made his way back to the courtyard where they had first arrived and found the men all settled around a cooking fire drinking mead already. The night was cooling down as the sun had gone below the horizon. In the background he could see two boys busy turning spits with two large goats stretched across the fire pits. They were roasting nicely and smelt delicious! "All set for a good dinner then?" he asked, and the men nearest to him all grinned and nodded enthusiastically.

He was a good leader and the men looked up to him and respected him, but more than that they admired him, as he took a personal interest in each man, and was good to them, treating them with respect in turn. He hunkered down by Julius and checked in with them to see how their day had been, and to explain the plans for the morrow. He noted that Matthew was sitting apart from the group and was chatting with one of the servant girls. She was a local from the region. Max let him be, and said to Julius: "How is the Taxman doing? Keep a close eye on him, I don't need any trouble on this trip, we have enough of that back in the barracks at Caesarea! Unfortunately we need him to communicate with the local peoples in their dialects, and for him to log the taxes, and note who has paid what! That is why we brought him on this trip. All that documenting is a headache, which he can have! As long as the money reaches the coffers for Festus, that is all that matters right now."

"Don't worry, sir," Julius replied, "We're keeping an eye on him. He's too nervous to make much trouble today. Besides, he's found a cousin to catch up with, see that girl over there? She's married to one of his cousins from his district. She is updating him on the local news!"

"Excellent! You are a great scout Julius! Keep up the good work, enjoy your evening meal, and I'll see you in the morning. Make sure that everyone is up and ready to depart first thing."

With that Max got up and left the courtyard, and headed back to the atrium to join the others. On entering the large, cool space of the atrium, he found Brutus and Maximillian had returned and were again lounging at the table, with goblets to hand. Julia was just entering with another lady, and they came to lounge at the table, and invited Max to take the other couch next to the host for the evening. "Right!" exclaimed Maximillian, "Now that we are all assembled, we can begin our evening's entertainment. Friends let me introduce you to Octavia, who is married to my cousin in Rome. She and her entourage have arrived early to prepare her household in readiness for the games. Octavia, these men are from my old barracks in Rome: Brutus and Max. Brutus and I have a long history of campaigns in the past! Okay, introductions over, let's get on with this evening. First we have some excellent repast for you, and then we have Fatima the dancing girl from Damascus! She is something else!"

He clapped his hands and the servants started to bring in plates piled high with roasted goat's meat, roasted duck and platters with grapes, pomegranates, figs and peaches. Brutus leaned over to his host, his mouth full, and nudges his friend, "Thanks Maxi, you have pulled out all the stops! This is such a treat after all these months working with these difficult people!" Octavia chipped in, "Oh do tell me what it is like here! I have only just arrived, and Julia has been so kind to arrange for our stay here. My husband Romano is still in Caesarea, as he has to arrange things for the delegation that will be arriving next month. It's all so different here, but this place is an absolute haven! It was so fortuitous to meet up with Julia in the market place in Caesarea last week. We were living in the same street in Rome when we were little girls!"

Julia smiled at her friend and turned to the men. "We have been so fortunate to find this place, and for Maximillian to have a reasonably sedate posting with mostly administration work, with some overseeing to be done for this town. I am looking forward to this festival that is coming up; to have some entertainment and to be in civilised company again! It does get boring here after a while!" "Well I don't know about civilised company but the local populace are a difficult bunch of people with strange laws and customs. They only worship one God and they keep holy days and feast days regularly! They also have celebrations coming up soon, but they are mostly not well educated, a bunch of goatherds and sheep carers! Like most peoples they have a few zealots that cause riots and uprising from time to time, but we deal with those kinds of people quickly and efficiently!"

They continued to chat and eat as the plates of food kept coming. Then Maximillian clapped his hands and a woman was brought in dressed in gossamer pantaloons and a short-cropped top, exposing her belly, which was decorated with small gold coins strung in a chain, hung around her tiny waist. On her head she had a red thin scarf also adorned with small gold coins. Her eyes were artfully decorated with kohl, which enhanced her exotic looks. She was heavily perfumed, and her fragrance wafted around the room. A young man followed her carrying a flute, and another young man came after him, carrying a lute. The two young musicians sat down and began to play a haunting melody. Fatima began to dance, slowly at first, with her belly vibrating as she undulated her hips in time to the music. The coins on her belly chimed softly as her belly muscles rippled. She also had bangles adorning both her wrists and ankles. As she clapped her hands in time to the music, the bangles jingled, adding to the rhythm as her feet moved swiftly across the floor. The music increased in tempo, and Fatima's dance intensified as her body rocked and swayed in response to the notes of the flute and the lute, The audience watched, fascinated, as she caught them up into her fantasy world, with the music and the perfume swirling around them all.

Slowly the music faded, and Fatima sank to the floor in a bow to indicate her performance had ended.

Maximillian turned to Brutus and asked: "Well! How was that?" "She would be amazing to play with!" Brutus said huskily, as he lusted after the dancer. Maximillian leaned closer to Brutus and whispered in his ear: "she could be yours if you desire, I have hired her for the night if she takes your fancy? I am sure you get little opportunity to indulge yourself in this awful place!" Brutus merely nodded; he didn't need to say another word.

Shortly after the guests departed to their rooms, Julia escorted Octavia out to show her to her rooms. Max turned to his host and thanked him for the evening, "Maximillian you have more than provided us a roof over our heads as we pass through your smallholding, you have been a wonderful and most generous host. It is much appreciated. I am sure Festus will acknowledge your generosity when he gets to hear of it!" "Ah ha, there are always ulterior motives my good man, " he said as he clapped Max on the shoulder, "You know that one good turn deserves another! A good word in Festus's ear will always be appreciated! I don't want to be left here forever, I am sure there are new postings coming up in Rome, and Julia for one, would love to be living back home again! I did hear that old Claudius had died and that a new governor was being discussed for his region down near Sicily! A posting back there would be just what we could do with! It's not that bad here, but she misses family and the culture and traditions of our own country! Well, good night my friends. Sleep well. I won't see you off in the morning, but safe journeys! Until we meet again." He walked out of the atrium, followed by Max.

Brutus took Fatima to his chamber.

CHAPTER 5

If you can dream it, you can achieve it!"

Zig Ziglar

Two years flew by as Caleb busied himself with learning a greater proficiency in weaving skills. Zillah watched Joshua grow and develop into a healthy, strong boy and their village grew in reputation. Boaz and Miriam produced more children, and the family business continued to grow and expand.

On the day that Caleb returned home he presented a new cloak to his wife: Zillah danced around the room in the new cloak that Caleb had made in beautiful blue wool. She smiled up into his eyes, "You are an amazing man, I love you so much. Look at you. You have turned ordinary wool into this beautiful cloak. Your skills have increased so much since you first took up weaving, and the time spent in Haifa was well worth it!" She reached up, cupped his face in her hands, and looked deep into his eyes: "It was hard having you away from home for so long, but now look at what you can do!" She did another twirl in the blue cloak, delighting in the fine weave and fall of the material.

She then took off the cloak and gently laid it on the loom. She looked up at her husband and asked: "Will you teach me how to weave like that too? We can then make more cloaks and tunics to sell at the big festivals, and it will mean that we can send Joshua to learn from that new teacher in Magdala! What do you think?" Caleb laughed with delight at his wife's enthusiasm, "My treasure," he said "our son is still only ten years old, he won't be able to go and learn under that teacher for at least four more years! Be patient, he is growing fast I know! As for teaching you weaving like this, not a problem! The more we share our skill the more we as a family benefit! You have also grown so much since you joined in the weaving with me; look at the cloaks you have been making whilst I've been away! It's so good being able to weave like this. Plus I haven't shown you yet, but I have brought back with me a young man called Adam. He and I have herded twenty sheep all the way from Haifa to our home. They have much finer wool, which is why I was able to make that fine blue cloak." He indicated the cloak lying across the loom.

"What's more, we will be able to get some of the local women here in town to learn how to spin for us, so that we can get on with the weaving. We will be able to experiment more now that I have also learnt to dye the wool with the purple and red dye colourings! We have already got the blue dye working out so well, so next we can make some blue tunics, which will be profitable in the next markets."

He put his arms around her and drew him into his embrace, "You are such a delight to me, and we are so blessed to have each other. Before you say it, yes, I know we would have loved more children, but I am so proud of you and Joshua, my precious little family!" He kissed her gently and then said: "Come, we must go and see where Boaz and Miriam are, and check on the children! I believe they are out in the hills nearby, as I saw John on my way to the house! I must introduce Adam to them, so he can join our shepherds, working with our goats and sheep!

They both put on their cloaks and Caleb picked up his staff and they headed out the door. Caleb was limping more heavily these days and needed the staff for support, his leg had never healed properly hence getting around was not so easy, so he often rode his little black donkey. They went round to the back of the house and fetched the donkey and headed off in search of the rest of the family. Caleb riding, and Zillah walking alongside him, with her hand resting companionably on his knee. He reached his hand down to hers and placed it lovingly over hers, she looked up and smiled at him. His heart missed a beat as he again thought of how much he loved her. As a couple they were both highly respected in the town. Caleb was often called in to advise and counsel on business matters and in family disputes. In fact, his name had been put forward: to be selected as one of the elders for their community.

Despite his time away in Haifa, he had established an excellent weaving business, and his garments were highly saught after, fetching good prices in the markets. Their goats were also thriving and had produced some excellent quality livestock, which they had developed into two large herds, keeping the whole extended family very busy!

It was a lovely Spring day, the sun was shining, but the day was not too hot, so they were glad of their cloaks. They climbed the small path up the hillside, and looked out along the horizon to scan for signs of the family or the goats. "Look, there they are, I can see Joshua sitting on the rocks swinging his legs." Zillah quickened her pace and led the donkey up the hill towards where she had spotted Joshua. At his feet there were several children squatting on the ground, playing with some stones they had found. Nearby were two shepherds. Zillah and Caleb approached them, and Caleb greeted them, "Hi Boaz and John, how are you both doing this fine day?"

Boaz turned and greeted his brother-in-law warmly: "Caleb, you're back! Great to see you. How was Haifa? What news do you bring? We have so much to tell you! All of us here are doing well; Miriam is over there cooking up some breakfast for us all, she has built a small fire in the lee of those rocks. She is being hindered more than helped by Naomi! The rest of our family are here as you can see!" Just then Joshua came running over, "Hi Papa, welcome home. Did you have a good trip? What was Haifa like? How long did it take for you to travel back?" He reached up and gave his father a big hug as much as he was able, so Caleb slid off the donkey and gave his son a bear hug in return. " Hi, son, so good to see you. You have grown so much!" Joshua grinned at his father, and then turned to his mother, "Mama did you bring any bread with you? I'm starving!" Zillah laughed at her son, "Just a minute, I'll pop over to see how Miriam is getting on with breakfast, I'm sure it won't be long!" she hurried over towards Miriam. Caleb chuckled at his son, "I see my son, you haven't changed a bit! Still needing to eat lots to keep that body of yours fuelled up!" He ruffled his son's hair affectionately, and turned to greet the other children as they came running over. "Hi, Uncle Caleb." They chorused, "When did you get back?" Caleb turned to them, "Hi Lizzie, Hannah, Gloria and who is this little feller?" "That's Ben," the children informed him. Boaz added, "Yes, Caleb, my son Ben was born just after you went on your trip to Haifa, he's nearly two now, and already thinks he is one of the gang here!" "Well," said Caleb, "How wonderful that you now have a son! A boy to carry on your family name!" "Yes," said Boaz proudly. "Already he is competing with Joshua for everyone's attention! See what I mean?" He laughed as he bent to pick up his small son, who had made his way over to his father's knee and was clamouring to be picked up by his Dad, so he could be in on the conversation from the vantage point of his father's arms. "He just wants to join in the big boys' stuff all the time!" Caleb laughed and reached out to hold the child, but Ben wasn't having any of it, "No!" he said as he pushed Caleb's hands away. Boaz reassured his son gently, "It's all right Ben, this is Uncle Caleb who has been away to learn new skills and is already getting acclaim for his work! It's thanks to Uncle Caleb that we are also in the family business and our goats are doing really well!" He turned to look at Caleb and said with pride in his voice: "This year we are expecting fifty of our goats to give birth soon, so we'll be kept busy over these next few weeks. Ha, Caleb, you've come back at just the right time to give us a hand as it's lambing season!"

Caleb laughed with Boaz, "I'm thrilled to hear your news! I was sure you could have handled it all quite well without me, as I see, you have been managing very well. John, how long have you been working with the family?" John looked over at Boaz as he answered Caleb, "I've been working with Boaz since last spring, and before that I was shepherding over in Galilee. My family is from Bethsaida, but I have travelled over this way to be nearer my sister and her family since our parents passed away. I was living with her and her family for a while, then I met Boaz at the markets, and he needed a shepherd, here I am! So far it has been a great experience, and now I have met the daughter of your cousin Elizabeth, and we are to be married next Tuesday!"

"Ah ha! I have truly come back at the right time! Not only will I be around to assist with the lambing season, but will be here for a family wedding! Excellent! So, John, you are to marry Abigail? Wonderful news, I am sure that her parents are delighted to have such a good match. It will be a brilliant opportunity to catch up with all the family! Thank you so much for joining us in more ways than one! Welcome to the family! Our family is growing fast! I have also brought some extra hands with me, as I have hired a man called Adam, who also has a lot of experience with sheep. He will make a great addition to our group. He will join us shortly, as he and I have brought twenty more sheep with us from Haifa! I plan on expanding our business, as we need the finer wool for the garments we will make for the richer folk. Come Boaz, walk me around the herds and then I must go back to join my family for the evening meal! There is obviously a lot to be done!" Caleb got back on his donkey, waved to Zillah and Miriam who were still over by the fire preparing breakfast, and he and Boaz set off up the hillside to inspect the sheep and goats. "We'll be back before long!" he called over his shoulder as he rode off.

"So typical of the men to ride off without having breakfast!" Miriam complained, "Especially as I have spent the last half hour preparing it all!" "Never mind," Zillah consoled her, "the children will appreciate it! Look here they come now! I know that Joshua has been hungry for ages!" She laughed as they all came running over to the two women, and smiled at her son, "Trust you to have that inner knowing as to when the food is ready! Let everybody get their fair share! OK sit down on the grass everyone, and Miriam will dish it up for you." Miriam had a stack of wooden bowls at her elbow, and dished the hot soup into them, as Zillah handed out fresh bread to everyone. John and four other shepherds came over to share in the warming food. They ate it quickly and came back for more.

"Good thing I made a big pot!" exclaimed Miriam. "It's like feeding an army here!" "Well half of them are your family!" Zillah smiled warmly at her sister, "You have been so blessed with all your children. I hope that you are feeling proud of them all!" "Oh, yes! They bring joy to my heart. Ever since Boaz held Naomi in his arms, on the day she was born, he has been a new man. He said it was both holding Naomi in his hands that first morning, and something that Caleb said that triggered a deep stirring in his heart, and he has really made a huge effort to make us all into an amazing family, which is soon to expand again!" "No, Miriam, really? I am thrilled for you. How many months are you now?" "Oh, about four months I think, so we should have the baby in the harvest season!" Zillah looked at her sister, "I am over the moon for you. God has blessed you so much, and look how you have blossomed into Motherhood! You have really been a mainstay for your family, and it is obvious that your children adore you, well done!" "Well, Zillah, thank you! I was not sure whether I should tell you about this new child yet, as I was fearful again that you would be so jealous of me, having so many when you only have Joshua." Zillah looked at her sister thoughtfully, "Dearest Miriam, it has truly been delightful for me to watch your family grow and to see my beautiful sister become a fulfilled woman, with a growing family to care for. You have your work cut out caring for them all, and you are doing a wonderful job of bringing them all up to be a blessing to you and Boaz. And now you have baby Ben to carry on the family name! Wonderful! As for me, yes I would have loved more children, but I am content with my son Joshua, he is a joy to me. He is learning so quickly, and is even helping me with the weaving. Although it has been hard having Caleb away, we are very content with our lives. No, it's not always been easy, but we are making the most of what we have. Caleb's leg troubles him a bit, but he has learnt to do the weaving so well. It means he can work without having to walk miles as before when herding the flocks, when he could be out on the hills for days, as you know with Boaz. Yet that has all turned out well, as he is loving the outdoor life, and still manages some carpentering from time to time.

Caleb is thrilled with what he is doing with the livestock, and how he has managed to build the herd not only in numbers, but also in quality! It seems Boaz manages to find good grazing and keeps them healthy, and has developed animal husbandry skills second to none! He has done well!" "Oh Zillah, you are amazing, so selfless, and always looking out for the best in others. You know the day you had Joshua I was so jealous of you. Boaz was being really difficult, so demanding and critical of everything I did. I could never do anything right! Yet the night we had Naomi, he suddenly changed. He began to see that we as a family were a unit, he began to notice things in a different way, and his attitude towards me has changed. He has become an amazing father and husband! As you can see he not only takes pride in his work, but he loves all his children so much! We are indeed blessed! And now we have another little one on the way. I really don't mind if we have another girl or boy, as long as the child is healthy!"

Miriam had been tidying up all her cooking utensils as she had been talking, and now she stood up "Zillah, come, let's go back to my place and wait for our men to come back, sit with me a while! Come children, let's go back home!" Zillah also gathered up the bowls into a cloth, and tied them together, and picked them up to carry them back. "Come Joshua," she called, "we are going back to Aunty Miriam's, to wait for your father and Uncle Boaz to return from inspecting the herds." They all set off down the narrow paths towards the village.

CHAPTER 6

"With men this is impossible, but with God all things are possible."

Matthew 19:26

Caleb and Boaz herded their flocks towards the market area. It was the autumn festival and the biggest market of the season in Capernaum. People from miles around had come to sell their wares in the open markets; there were people, animals and stalls everywhere! Somebody was baking bread, so the smells of fresh bread mingled with the smells of animals, dung and the sea. "Come over here Boaz, let's set up our stall under this tree, and we can make a pen for the animals just there."

Caleb was riding his donkey and leading two other donkeys piled high with cloaks and tunics that they had woven over the last few months, in preparation for the harvest markets.

John was helping Boaz to round up their animals that they had brought to sell. He had been leading yet another donkey which was carrying panniers with materials to make the pens to hold the goats in to prevent them from wandering off! Plus he had fodder for the animals to keep them occupied whilst waiting for buyers to come and view them. They had to carry everything with them, as the market square was just an open space made available for this occasion.

Joshua ran up "Hey Papa, there is a man over there who is asking about your cloaks already! Come on, let's set up the stall, so you can start displaying your wares!" Caleb slid off his donkey and made his way to their space under the tree. They all began to assemble their stall with a covering to provide shade for the garments, the sellers and the customers. The noise level was increasing as more and more people and animals were arriving to join the throng. It was to be a week long festival, so everybody had brought some supplies for themselves. Caleb had brought Naomi and Joshua, along with their new aunty Abigail, to help with the cooking and provisions to keep them all going for the week! They had had to leave Zillah behind as she was heavily pregnant and could not travel, although not due yet for at least another month. Miriam could not travel either, as she was caring for her newborn son, who was only a couple of weeks old. Therefore the two sisters were left to keep an eye on things at home.

"Pass me the goatskins, so that I can cover this stall, and make it waterproof, as well as provide some much needed shade from this heat! Then we will set up the tent behind, so we can have somewhere for Abigail and Naomi to start cooking some food for us, I am so hungry right now I could eat a whole goat!"

"Here, Papa," said Joshua as he laughed at his hungry father! He handed over the goat skins one by one so that Caleb could build the canopy. Having set up the stall with the tent behind, they began to build the pen for the sheep and goats to be kept in. They placed a water pot in the corner, so that they could keep filling it up from the well. Joshua and Naomi were kept busy helping out with all the preparations, as well as fetching water for their cooking and to fill the trough for the animals.

Suddenly a troop of soldiers marched through the square, everyone hastily made way for them to pass, but one of the goat kids escaped and ran across their path. Quick as a flash, one soldier, dived, grabbed it, broke its neck and laughed, "Ha, we have been given supplies!" He hoisted it onto his shoulders as the troops swept passed and marched on. Caleb yelled out "Hoi, that's my goat, either bring it back, or pay for it!" and he made to go and stop them, but Boaz held him back. The leader of the soldiers reined in his horse violently, and stared down at Caleb. "Huh, scum, it ran into us. We're keeping it. Thanks for the donation!" He rode on past with disdain on his face.

"No Caleb, you don't want trouble, you heard how that Centurion Brutus and his troops were causing mayhem down in Jericho a couple of years ago. Well I'm pretty sure that was him on his horse! I saw him once before, he's aged a bit, but still a force to be reckoned with. Leave him well alone!"

Caleb drew a deep breath. "Thank you brother, you are right, we cannot afford to let these people get to us, we have our own lives to lead, and their attitude is not going to dictate how I react, or how I should live in fear of them! This week we will sell all our goods- livestock, cloaks and tunics, and we will go home with a profit, which will more than compensate for the loss of the kid! By the grace of God we are indeed blessed to have our own businesses and to have the opportunity of bettering ourselves." "Yes, that we are. You know that both our wives are either expecting or coping with a new born! We are blessed again! Also we have John and Abigail helping us here in the markets. They are a great addition to our family, which is still expanding. Now we have John's brother, Simeon, who has joined us to help with all the livestock! We now have enough animals to divide them all into three herds, and we need more shepherds to help care for them all! It all started with you, as you had the vision to do two ventures, and both have expanded beyond your dreams!" "Ah ha, you are so right Boaz. Since coming back from Haifa, so much has happened!" He paused as a potential customer stopped at their booth. "I need two cloaks for the winter, one for my wife, and this one for myself. Let me see; this one will do for my wife, and this one for me.

How much?" The haggling began, and Caleb indicated for the man to have a seat whilst they discussed the price over a cup of tea. Joshua was summoned to go and get tea for the customer, and the haggling banter progressed. "Boaz, could you get one of the kids to show our client here; the quality of our animals. Perhaps, good sire, you would need a good male kid to help your herds grow stronger as well?" Boaz went off to the animal pens and returned with a 5 month old, baby billy goat, and the haggling continued. Finally the client stood up, he was a heavy-set man and well to do in his village from further north. He laughed with Caleb and said, "You drive a hard bargain, my good man, but your cloaks are of excellent wool, and of high quality. And your goat is one of the finest specimens I have seen. He will certainly help my herds develop and grow stronger. We will agree on the price and will see how we fare in the coming months. Peace be upon you and your family." They shook hands and exchanged money for the goods, and the client called up a small boy to help carry his purchases.

No sooner had he left, than another man appeared. "Greetings to you my good men, I am looking to buy a cloak that will see me through some more winters. My last one is getting threadbare after my trips to Jericho and back. What do you have for me?" " Well, sir, let me see, how about this dark blue one? Made from the finest wool, from sheep up in Haifa? Would this suit you? What's your name, and where are you travelling to?" Caleb held up the dark blue cloak he had selected. "My name is Matthew, and I am a tax collector. I do quite a bit of work with the Romans, but I would really love to get a place of my own and settle down. Nevertheless, at least I have a job. Even though I am not the most popular guy in the world, I am able to afford a decent cloak for myself from time to time. This deep blue one is magnificent; it would be just the thing for me. How much are you charging for it?" "Well, Matthew, would you like a chat over a cup of tea? And we can discuss prices and news whilst we drink our tea?" " No thank you, Caleb, I appreciate your offer of hospitality, but I rather think it would be more beneficial for you to have a quick sale, rather than being seen with me for too long. No, I will pay your price and leave you to get on with the business of the day. I will enjoy and appreciate my new cloak. Many thanks. I will see you around no doubt, as I hear your reputation is growing around the district!" With that he left having paid a handsome price for the cloak. "Poor man", mused Caleb, "he can't even enjoy a cup of tea, for fear of someone else getting annoyed with him, because of his line of work. Thank goodness we are able to be simple weavers and shepherds. I'm definitely for the simple life!"

By the fourth day of the festival they had managed to sell all the goats and all the cloaks and tunics, except for one blue cloak. This was of exceptional quality, the last one that Caleb had made before coming away on the trip to the festival. He considered it to be his best garment yet, and was asking for a high price for it. Several merchants had looked at it, but no one would agree on the price that Caleb was asking for. He refused to sell at a discount, knowing that his work was exceptional and that the price he was asking was not extortionate.

A certain Greek merchant, called Kostas, kept coming back to look at the cloak, but was also not ready to pay such a high price for the garment. So Caleb called all his family and work-ers together, and said: "Right, we have all done really well. Thank you to all of you for all your help, each one of you has contributed to making this venture a great success. We have worked really well as a team, including young Joshua and Nao-mi here. I would like us all to pack up as much of our gear as we can. We can then enjoy the rest of the day looking around at all that the festival has to offer. John and Abigail you can have the rest of the day to yourselves, I will get us an evening meal from my friends over on the East side of the square. We will rest overnight and then we can load up and leave in the morning. We should be back home the day after tomorrow, in time for our evening meal. We should be able to travel a little more quickly this time, as we have less to carry. How does that suit everyone?"

John said: "Thank you so much, it will be great for Abigail and myself, as we 'll have some time to go and visit her cousins on the edge of Capernaum, down by the sea. We might even be able to bring back some fish!" Boaz added; "Sure, that will be fine with me. Can I leave Naomi with you and Joshua, so that I can go and visit a couple of friends around the market square. I will be back by mid-afternoon?" "Yes, that's fine. Joshua and Naomi can spend time with me here, and we'll try to find a buyer for this last cloak. Go off and have some fun, and we'll see you all later!"

He settled down on the stool they had brought with them, and called the children to him. "Right you two, go and get some drinks from that stall just across the way there, where they are selling that delicious goat's milk drink which is so refreshing. Get three and bring them back here, and we can sit back and relax for a minute and enjoy whilst we wait for the others to return, you have both worked really hard. Well done!" Joshua and Naomi hurried off to do his bidding, and soon were back with three wooden cups of goat's milk. "Here you are Papa, thanks so much for letting me come this year, it has been so exciting to be a part of all this." He waved his drink in a circular motion indicating the whole market square, and took a large gulp of it, leaving a white smear on his upper lip as he grinned at his father. Caleb laughed, "Look at you my son, so grown up, you've even got a moustache! Well it has been good to have you along; you will be coming of age next year. As you know your mother and I are hoping for a baby brother or sister for you soon, finally! So you will have to take on some more family responsibilities and help me with the herding and weaving. Actually you are already able to do a fair bit, as you have learnt a lot about weaving from your mother. She has taught you well, whilst I was away!" "Yes, Papa, I am a quick learner, or so mother says But I would also love to do some carpentry. Perhaps I could learn some of that from Uncle Boaz? I love the rocking chair he made for you and mama all those years ago when I was a baby! I would love to be able to make things like that." "Ah ha my son, you have some drive and ambition I see, well done! That is a good idea, you can ask Boaz when he gets back if you can be apprenticed to him in his carpenter's shop, so that you can learn those skills right after your coming of age ceremony! And what about you young Naomi, what ambitions do you have?"

" Well, Uncle Caleb," she said shyly, "I am not used to having the opportunity to share my opinions with others, but I have been thinking that I would like to learn weaving from Aunty Zillah! Obviously I have seen how hard she works, but I would like to learn those skills as well! Yes, I am a typical girl; of course I would like to get married one day. But not yet! I want to be able to do other things as well!" "Good for you Naomi, so glad you were able to express your hopes and dreams. I believe in you. I will talk to Zillah when we get back, providing your papa agrees! I think the more weavers we have in the family, the larger our business possibilities become!"

Just then Kostas returned to their booth; "Caleb, my good man, peace be upon you!" They exchanged pleasantries and Caleb indicated for the big man to have a seat. "Naomi, please could you get us some tea? I have some things to discuss with Kostas here" The merchant leaned forward and said to Caleb: "I have been thinking about how I can do a good deal with you? How about I buy the cloak off you for a set price, and I will take the girl as well, so she can marry my son?" Naomi gasped and ran to hide at the back of the tent behind the booth." Caleb calmly turned towards his son, He indicated to Joshua to go and get some tea for him and the Greek merchant.

"Well Kostas, I know that you want to buy my cloak for your lovely wife. She is most certainly worthy of such an exquisite garment and she will be the talk of the town! I spent eighteen months learning from the very best in Haifa, as you know! And you know that I consider this to be my finest work to date. I am sorry my friend, but I am not selling for a lower price. I know the value of my work now, and my lowest price is what I will stick to, no less. As for my niece here, she is not yet of age. Besides, she is part of the family business, and she is still learning our trade. So I thank you for you flattering offers, but I must say no to both your proposals."

Kostas looked at Caleb for a few moments, frowned, and then said; "You'll be sorry you did not sell to me, be it on your own head!" With that he got up and drew himself up to his full height, and walked off without another word.

Joshua came back with tea, "What's up with him?" "Well," said Caleb, "I think we have just crossed paths with someone who is used to getting his own way, he is not used to people standing up to him". He did not say more, but was troubled by the implied threats from the merchant. Throughout the rest of the day, the children were sent on short errands, to buy various items they needed at home. Men dropped by to chat with Caleb all the time, one man warned Caleb to be careful of the Greek merchant and the Roman Centurion. He had seen the exchange about the goat on the first day, and was concerned for Caleb's safety. Other vendors warned Caleb about the Greek as they said he was a powerful merchant from up North, and one not to be crossed. John reinforced what these men were saying when he and Abigail returned from their excursion to the other side of Capernaum. "Hey, Caleb, you know what they are saying around the markets about Kostas your friendly Greek? He is a ruthless man, and will do anything to get what he wants. Apparently he has three wives up North, and has his fingers in lots of pies both with local merchants and with the Roman Government! You need to be careful and watch what you say!"

"Well," Said Caleb, "Technically I have not crossed him, I have simply advised him of the proper value of the cloak, and I am NOT selling myself short. I have worked hard at gaining my skill and getting my name known, why would I undermine myself now? My craft is of high quality. You won't find a better weaver this side of Jerusalem apart from myself. What's more he knows it!" "Yes" said John, "We know that, but if he wants something, he will really pull out all stops to get the things he wants. I will say again, please be careful, we love you and want our family business to continue to grow and be safe. I think you could appease him by giving him the cloak as a peace treaty so that we can keep on in our work and continue to grow both branches of the business; it will be a small price to pay to protect our families and our livelihood. Didn't you say he also had his eye on Naomi? Come on Caleb, you need to bargain for our safety, not just your pride in your expertise!"

Boaz returned during this exchange, and added his bit, "Yes, Caleb I agree with John, it's not just about the quality of the cloak, but the safety of our family. Look at it this way, it is an investment into our future, and if you can strike a peace treaty with him, maybe he will refer us to others so that your expertise will become more valued, as people recognise the quality of our products. Please see reason, not just for us, but also for our children."

Caleb listened to his kinsmen, and looked thoughtful for several moments. Then he took a deep breath, "Alright guys, I hear you. Yes, what price our safety? You are right, let's go and present him with the cloak as a gift. That way I have not undervalued the cloak, in fact I have made it more valuable in our eyes, as it will be a token of peace between us and him!"

He and Boaz left together with the cloak, and went across the marketplace to find Kostas. They found him outside his booth, chatting to a couple of Roman soldiers who were looking very much at ease with their Greek friend. As Boaz and Caleb drew nearer the soldiers left and Kostas suddenly noticed them approaching. "Ha Caleb the Cripple and his goat herdsman, what brings you here now?"

"Greetings Kostas." Said Caleb, "Peace be upon you and your family." And he then paused and waited to see if they were to be treated as guests in a polite manner or not. Kostas looked at them curiously. He then cordially invited them to enter his booth and to have a seat. He called a servant to bring some tea. "Come and sit down and have tea with me, and tell me what brings you to my booth? Let's not have hard feelings between us, OK?" They all sat down and Caleb calmly said, "Well Sir, your fame has gone before you, and I have heard that you are a merchant of great prowess. You have travelled far and wide and have seen great wonders!" He paused and looked at Kostas. The big man responded; "What you have heard is true. I have had the privilege of visiting many countries and nations in my life, and I have seen many riches, and exotic places. I have met kings and emperors, and have sat with them in high places. Equally I have met some of the scum of the earth and have learnt how to avoid conflict or deal with as necessary."

He looked at the two men sitting before him, he noted that Caleb was neither nervous nor afraid of him and was curious about their visit. He actually liked Caleb and Boaz, and admired their integrity. He suddenly decided that he was going to help them, so he listened with renewed interest to what they were saying. Caleb went on: "Well sir, I had also heard that you have been a very successful business man, and know that you have seen many wonderful things in your travels. I am curious as to why you have been so interested in my work, surely you have seen some exquisite cloths in the Far East?"

"Sure, I have seen gorgeous silks and other fine raiment in many places. I have traded with some of the finest silk merchants in the East." The servant brought them some tea, and poured it out for them, and left, bowing discreetly as he went. Kostas continued, he liked having an audience to show off to: "At my home in Tyre, I have some of the finest silks you can find, which is all well and good if it is a lovely warm day! My house looks out over the ocean and I can see some of my ships coming and going, bringing me goods from many places. The sea breezes play across my patio, and my wife and I enjoy entertaining elaborately when we can, I have traded in some of the finest spices, as well as marble, Arabian horses and riches from far flung places. Yes, my friends, it is true, I have seen much in my time!"

"So," Said Caleb, "Being as you are so widely travelled, I was wondering how it is that you visit our small market here? You have brought only a few of your wares, which I believe you have sold for a good price. Then you have come across to my small humble booth: and have liked my weaving?"

"Yes. On the days when the storms ride in over the sea, silk does not keep one warm! I have found that woollen garments are more useful. But often they are coarse and prickly, which irritates the skin, and makes them uncomfortable to wear. But you have managed to make the weave so fine, that the fabric feels smooth and soft. My wife loves to feel warm and comfortable and your products will meet her requirements nicely!" Caleb took a sip of his tea, and looked at the Greek merchant and smiled at him kindly; "Well sir, I am still adamant that I will not lower my price, as I know that I have managed to produce a garment of excellent quality." Again he paused, and then said: "I am flattered at your interest in my work, and am delighted that you appreciate my efforts in producing garments of high quality. So I would like to offer this blue cloak to you as a gift. I humbly ask that you will accept this as a token of good will from my family to yours?"

Kostas looked admiringly at Caleb, "I am surprised at you. You've obviously heard about me on the streets, yet you come with courage and boldness to offer your highly prized cloak as a token of goodwill! You have guts and determination. You know your worth, and are not willing to make compromises by selling yourself short, and you have integrity. All good qualities that I admire! I accept your cloak as a token between our families. I see that you are young and new to trading for big deals, as you have not made any demands on me or given me any provisos. I think I could teach you a lot about business and we might be able to work out some deals together, if you are willing to learn from me? You will find me a tough master, as I drive a hard bargain. On the other hand I respect hard work, good quality and honesty."

"Sir, that is most kind of you, and I appreciate your interest in my craftsmanship. I have not long returned from training in Haifa, where I learnt and honed my skills as a weaver. I would be happy to make a deal with you to make so many garments per year for you to sell on, if that would be agreeable to you?" "Now you're beginning to talk my language! Yes, I think that a deal could be arranged. How about we start with a consignment of twenty cloaks and ten tunics by the next big festival in Jerusalem? I will be there then. That should give you about six months. Can you make that many garments in that time?" Caleb responded: "Thank you sir, that is most generous of you, we will be able to produce that many garments by then, if we work hard. We look forward to meeting up with you in Jerusalem!"

"Well, Caleb, we better discuss some of the finer details of our deal. You may have heard some rumours about me in the market place, not all of them are true. I think that we will get on fine together. I look forward to being able to help you distribute your wares and to building your reputation. Your name will soon be famous up and down the country!" They spent the next half an hour discussing details of the deal and finally the men stood up to leave, Caleb and Boaz bid farewell to Kostas and gave him a blessing. A strong friendship had been forged.

Caleb and Boaz entered their tent where John, Abigail and the children were waiting for them. "Ha the venturers have returned! What happened?" John asked. Boaz smiled and waved his hand at Caleb, "This man is truly blessed!" "We struck a bargain with him, for us to supply twenty cloaks and ten tunics by the autumn festival in Jerusalem! I am still cautious as to his motives towards our humble family, but he genuinely seems to want to help us! We need to get a move on! Joshua you are going to have to start to learn the fine weaving skills now, as we will need all the help we can get to produce that many garments as well as have other stock to sell by the next festival, which is only a few short months away! Plus we have all the livestock to deal with. So we are going to be very busy!" "OK let's settle down, get some sleep and then head back home in the morning. We have work to do!" Boaz reminded everyone of their duties for the morning and they all settled down to sleep.

CHAPTER 7

"Whoever loves much, performs much, and can accomplish much, and what is done in love is done well."

Vincent Van Gogh

A month later Caleb rushed around to Boaz's house. "Quick, can you send Naomi to get the midwife, the baby is coming! Joshua is out in the fields with John, and I must go and get Abigail to come and help." Naomi wrapped a scarf around her head, and dashed out of the door and down the street. Caleb paused to say to Boaz, "Thank you for all you are doing, it has been such a busy time since we got back from the market festival, so much to do! Zillah has been working flat out on her loom, and I have been working hard at mine, and we have not really had time to prepare for the baby! Well, I'll be back, if I may, to sit with you a bit, whilst we wait for the new midwife to help Zillah, and see that the Lord provides?" Without waiting for a reply he ducked out of the door and headed to John's house. He knocked on the door and called out, "Abigail, please come and sit with Zillah her time has come." The door opened and Abigail appeared with a big smile on her face, "Oh Caleb, how exciting for her, she has looked forward to having this child so much! After nearly twelve years since having Joshua, at last, a new little one for her!" They hurried back to Caleb's house and Zillah's mother appeared at the doorway. Anna stopped Caleb, "Don't worry Caleb, she will be in good hands, just wait until we send for you. Come Naomi, you can give me a hand." They both entered the humble dwelling and shut the door. Caleb turned and made his way back to Boaz's house. "Hey, Boaz could you fix me a large drink of tea and some breakfast? I am starving and anxious and on edge like I have not been for ages!" Boaz led Caleb to the table, and called out "Miriam dear, could you get us some breakfast, whilst we wait for this new arrival?" Miriam appeared from the kitchen holding a chubby infant in her arms, "Yes dear. Lizzie and I are already busy in the kitchen preparing breakfast, and we can easily stretch it to add one more at the table." She smiled at Caleb, "are you excited now that you are about to have a new baby at last? I know that Zillah has been looking forward to this moment especially knowing we were expecting this little fellow when you got back from Haifa! Here Boaz, can you hold Simeon for a bit, and breakfast will be here shortly." She handed over the child, and bustled back to the kitchen.

"Hey Simeon," Caleb chucked Simeon under the chin. The infant looked up at his uncle and gave him a big smile. "I declare that you are fatter than yesterday! Do you know that you will soon meet your new cousin? He is growing so fast! Look how he is holding his head up and looking around, he is a chip off the old block alright!"

Boaz smiled, "Yes, he is doing well. We are so blessed with our brood. Now we have to concentrate on getting them to learn all our skills and abilities, so they can grow up and look after us in our old age! My mother isn't doing so well, she's at my sister's house in Tiberias. She is not moving much these days, and is being looked after by my sister, Rebecca, and some other elderly ladies in the village. They are coping well for the moment. I got a message from that lad who has been over there last week. He brought back messages for several folk in the village, as he has been around Galilee getting casual labouring work for the last few months. I was wondering if you wanted to take him on as an extra hand? The flocks and herds are growing, and you are too busy with your weaving to help much. I have had to be around here a bit more, what with little Simeon being so small, and Miriam having to do so much with the house, and all the children. So I have had to take on some more carpentry work to be closer to home! So what do you think? Could you use an extra shepherd?"

"Well," Caleb responded, looking thoughtfully at Boaz. "Sorry to hear about Debra, it's difficult with these elderly folk. When they get less mobile, it makes life harder for everyone. I'm sure Rebecca is managing, she is such a capable young girl. Isn't she married yet? As for this new chap, I'll have to meet him, and see how he works with the animals, how much experience has he had?"

Before Boaz could answer, Naomi came through the door, "Uncle Caleb, Anna says you must come now, Zillah has had a difficult time, but the baby is finally here, and you must come!" Caleb jumped up and grabbed his stick and made his way as quickly as he could to his house. He opened the door, and went in to find his wife surrounded by all the ladies: Anna, Naomi, and even the old midwife Shauna was there. "Hello, what's happening?" They turned to see him as he walked in, and parted so that he could see Zillah lying on her bed, with a small bundle in her arms. She looked up as Caleb approached. "Look darling, our daughter is here, can we name her Johanna?" "What does that mean?" Caleb asked. "God is gracious" Zillah said. "For He has most certainly been gracious to us, look at our little miracle!"

"Excellent, then she shall be called Johanna." He sat down with a sigh, taking her into his arms he said: "Welcome little Johanna. We are so thrilled that you are joining our family, may you be blessed with health and wealth, love and joy throughout your life."

Turning to Zillah he lent over and kissed her on the forehead, "How are you? I hope you're not too tired, Naomi mentioned that you had not such an easy time of it this time. She is adorable and so worth all the wait! Now we are doubly blessed, as we have two beautiful children!" He looked at Johanna nestled in the crook of his strong arms, "She is just like her mother!" He cradled her for a few minutes more and then kissed her on her forehead too, "She is so strong and precious. You have done well, my love!" He handed the infant back to her mother, "Now get some rest, and I'll ask if Naomi can stay with you a while, to give you a hand whilst I am out with the boys sorting out the sheep and the goats for a bit. Then I will be back to keep an eye on you and continue to weave these new cloaks we have to make to fill our order for Kostas. We are being stretched at present. But it is good to be busy!"

Zillah gave a tired sigh, "Yes, my amazing man! Don't do too much. I know that we have a lot to do, but as you say, life is very full at present, yet it is good to be busy! Thank you for all you are doing, we will get there, persistence is the key! It's such a joy to have a daughter to share our lives with!" Caleb stood up and bent down to kiss his wife and daughter on their foreheads, "OK my two beautiful darlings, rest and sleep for a bit, Naomi will be around to help you, won't you Naomi? Thank you Anna and Shauna for all your help. I'll leave you to sort things out here, and will let Boaz know that you're staying here Naomi. We will be out and about for a bit, see you later." He picked up his stick and headed out of the door to join the shepherds.

CHAPTER 8

"In any given moment we have two options: to step forward into growth or to step back into safety."

Abraham Maslow

Life was full and busy as they all worked hard to produce as many cloaks and tunics as they could. Not just to fill the order for Kostas, but to have extra garments to sell in the markets in Jerusalem. The new way of weaving was producing a much better quality of cloth, and the new garments were definitely softer and of better quality than the rough weave that Caleb had started with. Zillah was not as free to do as much as she would have liked, but was loving looking after baby Johanna! They watched both baby Simeon and Johanna grow and develop, Simeon was already at the crawling stage and therefore spent a lot of time strapped to his mother's back, so she could get on with keeping the family provided for in bread and meals. It was the only way Miriam could keep him out of mischief!

But now attention was turning towards Joshua as he was nearing the time of his coming-of-age celebrations. "Mama, my teacher said that I must know all the Books of the Law before I can come of age!" "Son, all the boys in your class have to go through this ceremony, it is amazing that they can all do it, and I am utterly convinced that you can too! You just have to apply yourself! Get your father to remind you what the law is all about, and ask him to help you remember it all! You know you are almost one of the men now, so you need to do your share of the duties! Don't forget you are also now responsible for the three little lambs that we have bought that are being hand-reared. They will need feeding again shortly!" "Oh yes, Mama, I know. They are so cute; the little black one almost sucks my fingers off in his enthusiasm to get at the milk! I love looking after them, they are all so greedy, and as they suck they flick their little tails, it is such fun. All three of them are so different!"

"Well that is so like children, each one of you is unique! And each one of you is loved so much! Right now, I am busy with this weaving, but shortly I will be cooking our evening meal. Your father and Uncle Boaz will be here for a meeting to discuss who is going on the next business trip, and to help you be ready for your test!"

"OK Mama, I'm off now to feed the lambs, and then to find Papa to get him to help me with all my questions! See you later, love you." He ran out of the door and over to the small barn they had at the rear of their property where they were housing the lambs. He ran to get a bucket, and then over to the she goat that was the one they were milking at present. He patted her and then squatted down beside her and began to squirt her milk into the bucket. As soon as the lambs heard the milk they began to make bleat loudly, as they knew that food was coming their way. Joshua laughed, "Be patient, it's coming!" he called to them.

Joshua quickly fed the lambs with the fresh warm goat's milk, dipping his hands into the milk and letting the lambs suck the milk from his fingers, their little tails wagging the whole time! Then he hurried off to find his father and his Uncle Boaz. He found them at the rocks just up from behind the barn, where they were standing looking out at the sheep and goats now straying across the hills together. John, Adam and the other two men were in a group all looking out over the fields, studying the flocks. Caleb saw Joshua coming and put his arm around his son's shoulders and looked at him proudly, saying with great affection, "Well, my son, how are those little ones doing? I am hoping that we can breed from that little ram so that we can get some finer wool for the future. Hopefully the two ewe lambs will also become good mums and give us lots of healthy special wool lambs for the future. We are watching our flocks grow and multiply in leaps and bounds. What do you think?" "Oh Papa they are doing so well, the little ram is very greedy and butts at my hand all the time, and tries to take all the milk for himself! He is already taller than the other two!" Caleb laughed and indicated to the other men, "We'll make a shepherd of him yet! Look at our fine new kids, four of them playing over there with their doting mothers, who are keeping an eye out for them as they crop the grass. They will certainly help our herds to develop well, they are all strong and healthy and showing good markings. We are a great team!" Adam added, "Yes, I have so much to be grateful for, since joining your team I have learnt so much from you men. How to really care for the animals, and also how to respect and treat people. You are a great mentor to me, and I also have had the privilege of meeting Rebecca on several occasions, and well, you know Boaz, I really like her, and was wondering if you would consider allowing me to become your brother-in-law?"

Caleb laughed with delight; "David joined us and then really became part of the family when he married Abigail, and now you want to make a match with Rebecca! I will have to have a word with the town matchmaker, as she will think that I have taken over her job! What do you think Boaz, a new addition to the family?"

Caleb put his hand on his brother-in-law's shoulder as he grinned up at his friend. The men all looked at each other and laughed together, Joshua joined in just because it felt good to be included in the men's banter. Boaz turned to Adam with a twinkle in his eye, "Well, seriously Adam, you haven't wasted much time have you? How often have you seen my sister? She's a good, hard working girl, and is devoted to my mother, who, as you know has not been so well of late. Rebecca can't really leave her at the moment. I will have a discussion with her and see what she thinks. I know that is not the norm for our culture, but I have to think of my mother as well." "Oh, yes I totally agree, I would want her to continue to look after your mother as well. I actually got talking to her a few times in the village where she lives now, as I was there working as a labourer getting work where I could, whilst I was travelling around. My family were all killed in a fire a couple of years ago, since then I have been looking up relatives near Cana, but no one had work for me. So I have been on the road and learning what I can from different people I meet along the way. I met your sister at the well, and helped her with her water jars. She and her friend were both there. Her friend had just dropped her jar and it had smashed against the well wall. I simply went over with a jar I had with me.

Actually your mother's sister and my mother were second cousins! So in fact I am related, as my great grandfather was Jonathan from Cana!"

He drew a big breath and went on: "I was talking to David at the village gate last week, and he said that there is a small cottage just come up for rent on the East side of town, which has two small rooms. We could start life there, and there would be room for Debra as well!"

"My goodness, you have been busy! Of course I have heard of Jonathan of Cana, but had never met the man!" exclaimed Boaz, "give me a couple of days and I will go over and visit my mother and sister, and will get back to you after that. Fair enough?" He reached across and slapped Adam on the shoulder. "You are a fast worker my lad, and are already proving yourself as part of the team. I am delighted that you are actually family! It will bring joy to my mother's heart to have a husband for Rebecca so there will be someone to care for her after my mother has passed on."

"Wow, that would be brilliant! Since arriving here I have at last found people that I can feel comfortable with. I have work that looks likely to grow and develop into so much more. And I have found someone with whom I can share my life! Life at last has meaning and purpose! Thank you so much. And thank you to Caleb for all that you and your family have done for myself and the people in the town, as you have been so gifted in setting up business opportunities. You have managed to get employment for so many people: the two sisters next to the cottage I was looking at are now spinning your wool as fast as they can. Now Seb and his brother Ben have been able to set up their dyeing operation, and are learning new colours instead of just the natural greys and browns most commonly seen around here. So the town is getting a name for itself! You have been such a blessing, and it is helping us all to be able to gain respect and have better work prospects even in this tiny township!"

Caleb shifted his weight to get more comfortable, his leg ached so much these days, and it was not getting any better. "Well thank you Adam for your kind words. I kind of had to look around after I had had a fall in which I seriously damaged my leg, as you know. I was out on the hills over near Chorazin, chasing a wolf that had got one of my best kids, and I stupidly caught my foot in a hole. I fell awkwardly and I heard a snap. I was able to use my staff as a splint and somehow managed to get back to the rest of the flock. I lost that kid to the wolf, but saved the rest of the herd. Somehow I got myself, and the flock back to Capernaum and was able to do a deal: in exchange for two of my goats I got a donkey. Using that method of travel enabled me to herd the flock back here to Nain. Life was tough for a while, but Zillah was able to help and support me to get my flocks looked after by a lovely old man called Seth. He has since passed on, but he was a real godsend. He taught me so much about herding. Ever since then my leg has never been straight. So obviously I was not able to get about the hills so freely anymore. Then I discovered weaving, and have been learning more all the time. It means I can still support my family, without having to trudge over the hills, and now Zillah is becoming a skilled weaver, and even young Joshua here can make a garment if he puts his mind to it!" He smiled at his son. "Well lads, it's been quite an eventful afternoon! I have to help Joshua with some questions. His big day is coming up and I want him to be ready! See you for supper tonight! Come Joshua, fetch my donkey and we'll be off home!"

CHAPTER 9

"Successful people are always looking for opportunities to help others. Unsuccessful people are always asking: 'What's in it for me?'"

Brian Tracy

Five months later, after much hard work, Caleb, Boaz and Joshua were again on the road. This time they were headed for the markets in Jerusalem. During the family discussions it had been agreed that the two men and Joshua were to make the big journey to Jerusalem leaving behind their wives and other children. The other men were to shepherd and supervise the flocks and herds. Zillah was left to not only supervise the ongoing weaving and spinning, but to carry on the family business. Caleb had three donkey loads of garments and one donkey load of provisions for the journey. They had had word from Kostas that he would meet them in Jerusalem, and that he would take delivery of the garments he had ordered.

Joshua had had his coming of age celebrations and was now considered a part of the family business. He delighted in learning as much as he could from his father, and was already showing promise as a weaver. Today he was running ahead of their group with lads of his own age. Their small party had joined up with other merchants and travellers to make a caravan of about one hundred people all heading for the big festival, and to participate in the ceremonies in Jerusalem. There was safety in numbers, as marauding bands and robbers were increasing in the region due to the oppressive taxes and heavy-handed Roman regime.

Caleb was riding his faithful little black donkey and leading another one with the special consignment of garments for Kostas. Caleb shouted over to Boaz, who was leading three donkeys as he travelled on foot behind Caleb. "Boaz, did you see where Joshua went?" "Yes, he has gone up front with Nathan's boys. The three of them have joined up with several others and are having a great time together. I reminded him to be back with us at our next stop, so he can help with the donkeys and getting the fire going so we can heat up water for our drinks and to cook something!"

"Excellent! He is really taking his duties seriously, I am so proud of him. Did you see that cloak he helped me to make? It is one of the finest I have made, and the new blue dye is exceptional! I have left that particular cloak at home for Zillah to have, so that she has something to keep her warm this year. Johanna is growing and developing nicely, I am also so proud of her! As I know you are of your girls and Ben and baby Simeon!" "Yeah, my lot are like mushrooms, blink and they have become a head taller! Ben is now walking around and helping with the chickens! He tries to catch them in his chubby little hands!"

"Hey!" Boaz exclaimed, "look over there? Isn't that a whole group of people coming in from the West? It is going to be packed in Jerusalem. And behind them there is a large dust cloud coming up on their heels!" "Yes you're right, and I bet that dust cloud is a group of Roman soldiers coming from Caesarea, they will probably be bringing in reinforcements to keep an eye on everyone, as we all congregate together for the big festival. See how the outriders are riding horses? We will just have to practice keeping out of their way as much as we can, at least this year we won't have to worry about our livestock running in front of them!"

"Ha, yes, but we must also be wise in our dealing, I am not sure about this arrangement we have with Kostas." Boaz chipped in: "He could be the making or breaking of us! If he sells our garments and the quality is approved, we will be making a name for our selves far and wide, bit if not, well we could be in deep trouble!"

"Enough Boaz, yes, I know we must be cautious, but we have to trust he will be honest in his dealings with us, after all, if he is able to sell on our garments for a good profit, he will need some more stock!"

Caleb suddenly noticed a man riding his camels just ahead. "Oh I do believe that I have just seen Jason, that apothecary from near Magdala. I met him on my travels on my way to Haifa. Let me just trot ahead for a minute, follow me and stay close, we mustn't get lost in this crowd!"

He pulled his donkeys over to the gap ahead, and trotted up to a man riding a large camel, and leading a second one laden with two panniers hanging on either side of the camel, with the contents covered with bright red rugs to keep out the dust. "Hello Jason, how is life with you?" The man turned his head to see where the voice was coming from. He was a strong man, with broad shoulders, and had laugh lines etched into his face. He had large brown eyes and a ready smile. He looked down and saw Caleb.

"Caleb! What are you doing here? How's that leg of yours?"

"Not so bad, not so bad. Life is good, I have done a lot since I met you on the road up to Haifa a couple of years ago! I am off to the markets in Jerusalem to sell my wares, and obviously to join in the festival, I have become a weaver of growing repute!"

"Well congratulations! Actually I had heard that you had developed some weaving skills, and I heard that you have now got a young man called Adam working with you. I met him a couple of years ago, after I had seen you on the road! It was not long after his family had been destroyed by fire. He was a lost soul for a bit, but I was able to comfort him and advised him to travel a bit, and to gain some life experience, before the good Lord showed him where to settle!" "You know Adam? That man never ceases to surprise me! Yes, it's true he now works for me, and got married recently to my brother-in-laws sister, Rebecca. They had got her mother Debra with them, but having got her settled in the cottage with them, she became ill and died just last month. They are still mourning her loss, but also rejoicing, as now they are expecting a baby sometime in the spring!" "Wonderful news! I am so pleased for him. I knew his family before the tragedy of the fire, and was concerned for his welfare. News travels, but mostly the bad stuff! The good stories have to wait to be told on journeys like this, where we meet up with fellow travellers and snippets of news get passed on! I myself, have been continuing on as a peddler of medicines, and have had some success with bringing health to the sick. I don't know if you heard about the widow from Cana? I managed to bring about a cure for her from falling down sickness, and so my prowess as a successful healer and producer of genuine medicines that treat the cause is growing. I have supplies here to sell in Jerusalem as well. I also have something in my baskets here, which will help the pains in your leg. If you like I can get you some at our next stop for the night?"

"That would be much appreciated, thanks so much. You must join us for a bite to eat; we will enjoy your company! My brother-in-law Boaz is with me, and my son Joshua. We would be delighted for you to share what we have. It's a long journey, and you must find it a challenge travelling by yourself?"

"Yes and no! I like my own company and am able to look after myself mostly! As you know, I have practiced medicines and also exercises to build my body strength. I am sure I explained that to you the last time we met? I taught you how to build your muscles in your leg, even though it had not healed properly. It was too long ago for me to help you with your bone formation, but at least you are able to use that leg still and get around! I continue to do my daily routines, as well as to develop my medicinal knowledge and skills no matter where I am. And thank you, I would enjoy some company and look forward to meeting the other members of your family. It is a long road, but hopefully a worthy journey."

Caleb indicated behind him, towards Boaz. "Over there, lead-ing three donkeys, is my brother-in-law, Boaz. My son Joshua is right up at the front with some of his friends, but we will enjoy having more time to relax and share over the evening meal together. Thank you for accepting my humble invitation to join us this evening."

"The pleasure is mine!" Jason smiled down at Caleb and rode on, swaying with the motion of his camel's steady pace. Boaz and his donkeys drew along side Caleb, as Caleb's donkeys slowed back to a walk. The donkeys were relieved not to have to keep trotting so much.

Finally the caravan drew aside for the night. Everyone pitching a tent and lighting a camp-fire in order to cook their evening meals, so their hunger could be satisfied after the long march of the day. Caleb and Boaz settled their donkeys, putting their packs carefully inside their tent, and getting the fire going. As the lentil stew was being cooked, Joshua came running up, "Hi Papa, Uncle Boaz, this is my friend Mica. Can he share with us? His family are over there, about twenty tents away, and there are too many of them, so would that be okay?" A stocky lad with a cheeky grin came up alongside Joshua as they both looked enquiringly at Caleb.

"Sure son that would be wonderful. Before we eat, could you both go and get some water from the well? We also have a guest joining us tonight: the apothecary/healer I told you about, who helped me on my journey to Haifa, he will be with us soon. Oh look there he is, making his way over towards us" Caleb worked quickly and efficiently as he put the kettle over the fire, to heat up and stirred the lentil stew he was making in another pan hanging from a sturdy stick over the fire. Jason came up leading his camels, and made them sit down so he could take their packs off. He then tethered them nearby and put his goods into Caleb's tent.

"Welcome my friend, come rest your weary limbs over here, we will be able to eat shortly. Would you like a drink first?" Caleb passed a cup of goats' milk to Jason and settled back to wait for the stew to cook. "Thanks I appreciate that, it is good to relax with friends after a hard days travelling!" "Yes, we need time to sit back and relax a bit, as there will be another day of travelling to look forward to tomorrow! Make yourself comfortable Jason, I'm just getting something for you." Caleb got up and went into the tent behind them; he rummaged around a bit and came back out carrying a beautiful blue cloak. "Here Jason, I would like for you to have this as a thank you for all that you did for me in the past, and as a token of our friendship, which I hope we will enjoy for many years to come!" Jason took the cloak and felt the quality of the cloth. "Wow, Caleb, you didn't have to do this you know, but thank you, I really am most grateful for this. My old travelling cloak is getting quite threadbare. This one will be able to keep me warm nicely! I see what you mean about your weaving skills, this is a fabulous cloak, and the colour is stunning. When I wear it I will remember our friendship!"

The men sat around the fire and began to discuss the journey, the current situation and their hopes for the coming festival. Joshua and his friend Mica went to get water from the nearby well, and to ensure that all the donkeys were tethered safely, with fodder for them to eat. After their evening meal, the men talked long into the night, before they all got their cloaks and wrapping themselves in them, made themselves comfort-able around the fire and went to sleep. Except for Caleb, who slept in the tent to guard the stock and other goods they had brought with them.

CHAPTER 10

"I have been impressed with the urgency of doing. Knowing is not enough; we must apply. Being willing is not enough; we must do."

Leonardo da Vinci

On the third day the caravan arrived in Jerusalem. The journey had been hot and tiring, but finally the travellers had let out a cheer on seeing the walls of Jerusalem appear in the distance, as they crested the hills surrounding the famous city. By this time, the friendship between Jason, Caleb and Boaz has been firmly established; they had all agreed to support one another, and to work alongside each other whilst in the city. Many other travellers had joined their caravan, swelling it to twice its size. There was a strong Roman presence, as foot soldiers marched in small platoons observing the crowds, keeping an eye out for troublemakers. As they came by, everyone moved to get out of their way, they were known to have quick tempers and short fuses!

Jason took his camels to some stabling at an inn on the outskirts of the city, as there was not room to take the camels into the narrow streets of Jerusalem. By the time that Jason had reappeared, Caleb and Boaz had dispersed their packs onto three of their donkeys, as it was not much further to carry everything, and helped Jason to unload his panniers onto their fourth pack donkey. This enabled them to get all their gear into the city.

They all then wound their way through the narrow streets to a place that Jason had reserved in advance, having used it in previous years, as he knew the owners of the house nearby. He advised his travelling companions to set up their booth next to his stall, right by one of the main thoroughfares of the city. The donkeys were relieved of their burdens and Joshua and Boaz took them all back to the stable in Jason's friend's courtyard, off the main way. The apothecaries were all selling their wares in one section, with various other merchants selling their products and wares in close proximity, which suited Caleb and Boaz well, as they were near enough for them to share watch with Jason over their stalls.

There were still two days to go until the seven-day festival actually commenced, so there was time to lay out there garments and then for Caleb to take Joshua to visit the temple. "Come on Joshua, let's head over to the temple where we can offer our sacrifices and you can see for yourself the wondrous sights of the this most holy place and its surroundings!" They passed through the narrow streets, which then opened up into a broad highway leading up to the temple. Joshua stopped and looked in awe at the massive building: "Wow, Papa, how long did it take them build such a huge place? Look at the size of the stones in the walls! How on earth did they get them here? I feel so small!" His eyes were open wide as he gazed around him, overwhelmed by the sights and smells of the huge building.

Caleb laughed with delight at his son's wonder, "Yes, my son, it is huge. It did take a long time to build, but let's go inside and offer our sacrifices, and pray for a great future for you!" They entered into the men's courtyard where there was much activity. They exchanged their money and bought a lamb to offer as their sacrifice. Joshua was all eyes and ears as he took in the scene before him. So many people! Smoke rising up from the burnt offerings, the smell of incense over the place, people praying; so much going on!

Caleb put his arm around his son's shoulders, "Look, over there; my son, see the doorway at the top of those steps? That is the entrance to the Holy of Holies. Only the High Priest can enter once a year! It is such an awesome place! I have only been here a few times in my life, but I am thrilled to be able to bring you here today. You have made me a very proud father, bless you my son. I love you so much, and it swells my heart with pride to watch you grow and develop into a fine young man. Over the next five years I hope that you will learn as much as you can from me, and become an even better weaver than myself! I will also need your help in supporting your mother and your little sister. I so want you to have more opportunities and advantages than I did! We will then have to start looking around for a good wife for you!" "Oh no, Papa, I couldn't become as good as you, but I'm learning as fast as I can! I am also not ready to be married yet! Loads more to learn yet!" Joshua looked up into his father's eyes and glowed with pride as his father blessed him, Caleb squeezed his sons' shoulders, "Yes my son, I know that you are a quick learner and you are doing really well. The local teacher has already taught you all he can. It is time to step up and learn even more! You have a destiny to fulfil!"

As they moved across the courtyard they bumped into a man in a blue cloak. "Why hello, isn't it Matthew? How are you? And what are you doing in Jerusalem?" As Matthew looked up into Calebs' face, Caleb noticed a difference from the last time they had met: "Matthew! What's happened to you, you look so different. You're not stressed anymore! You have an aura of peace about you?" "Hello sir, who are you?" "I am Caleb, the man you bought the cloak from, back in Capernaum about six months ago!" "Oh, yes, Caleb my good man, this cloak has been such a blessing to me! It is so warm, and has been admired by many. Since I last saw you my life has changed dramatically! I am no longer a tax collector! I follow the Teacher these days and we give to those in need. I love this life, helping others instead of extracting monies for the Romans!" "Well, that is a big change, but you certainly look better for it! My son and I are here to sell our garments in the market. Do drop by and visit if you have a moment. We are near the apothecary's section. Look for Jason the apothecary, our stall is right next to his." "Ah Caleb, these are troubled times that we live in, but it has been so good to change and learn about myself. Now I am finding a more fulfilled life, free from stress and anxiety: of which I had plenty as a tax-collector! Now I am with a group of like-minded people from all walks of life, we are here to help our neighbour to have a better life! Our neighbour is anyone in need! I wish you every success with your sales, and hope to catch up with you one day!" They bid each other farewell, and returned to their stall in the market area.

As they approached they saw Boaz talking to two men. Jason was also busy with customers, mixing up some lotions using his pestle and mortar, making up some specific cure to meet the customers' needs. Then Caleb saw a man and his wife approaching their booth. Two men who were guarding them were clearing the way for these two prosperous people to pass. The lady, who was finely dressed and wore a lingering perfume, had a maid at her side. The lady paused at their stall and began to examine the garments. She shook one out and held it up against her maid to get a good look at it. The man, a rich merchant, gestured to Caleb, "Hey, my good man, I hear that you are Caleb the Cripple. I have it on high recommendation from Kostas, my good friend from Tyre, that you are an excellent weaver! He has informed me that you have a special consignment for him, which he will be picking up in four days time. He will be with us where we are staying, at the fort. We would like to see those garments as he advised me that we could purchase one from him. My wife, Priscilla, here, needs a special new tunic to wear at the Emperors' banquet next week. I see that you have some of the finest woollens that I have seen in a while."

"Why, thank you good sir, and please pass on my thanks to Kostas for his good word. I hope that your lady will find something that will please her? Allow me to show you a couple of the garments that I have set aside for Kostas." He went to the back of the stall and opened one of the packs enclosing the consignment of garments and withdrew 3 tunics for Priscilla to inspect. "Here, my lady, would one of these suit your taste?" "Well, young man, you have certainly got some rare talent! I have not seen such fine woollens as these, this side of Tyre. My husband also travels extensively, and has brought me back some exquisite items from his journeying, but I have rarely seen such colours. You have managed to give the dyes some subtle hues to these garments, and the finest of the weaves makes the fabric so soft, and they hang beautifully!" Caleb bowed to her, "Why, thank you for your kind compliments, I have still so much to learn, but it is a joy to work with the wools that we are harvesting from our flocks back home. We are establishing a good flock, thanks to the help of a great team!" The merchant turned again to Caleb, "Well you have certainly lived up to your reputation; if you get such an accolade from my lady here! She is an expert in fine quality garments! Well dear, which one is it to be?"

Priscilla replied: "I would like to have these three garments sent to our chambers at the fort, so that I can try them on in comfort, and then decide which one I like best. Would that be alright with you young man?" Caleb not used to this approach, looked at Boaz for confirmation: "We could arrange that, don't you think? I am sure that we could arrange for one of us to deliver the garments to the villa later this afternoon. Would that suit my lady?" Boaz gave a quick look at Caleb, but said nothing in front of the merchant.

The awkward moment was saved when the merchant himself stepped in and said: "Ah, no, actually we are away for the rest of the day. We need to get out of this throng and are visiting the palace out at Herodian. We will be gone for a couple of days. Could you send them over in the afternoon of the fourth day from now? Kostas will be with us then, so we can buy the garment direct from Kostas? That way you will be fulfilling your assignment, and he will be able to sell one of the garments directly on to us immediately! It will be a most amicable agreement all round!"

Caleb looked relieved. He was pleased at having the pressure removed from an immediate delivery with added potential complications; in addition it gave him time to talk the matter over with Boaz and Jason.

"Yes, sir, I think that we could most certainly arrange that. That would allow time for your lady to try on the garments, select which one she prefers and we can leave the rest of the consignment with Kostas. That would work well for all parties."

The merchant looked pleased that they had arrived at a satisfactory agreement. "Yes, that will be excellent. We will see you in four days time. I will send a boy to come and collect you and show you where to come. Kostas will be with us and you can deliver the consignment to him at the same time. Very convenient! Right my dear, let's get out of this busy place and get some fresh air!" The merchant and his entourage left the stall, making their way through the crowds with difficulty.

"Well", Caleb exclaimed, "That was interesting. We have lots to learn about making arrangements for delivery and receiving payments and so on! We'll have to ask Jason for some advice regarding these matters; he has obviously had a lot of experience with his customers! Boaz could you please put these garments back with the others set aside for Kostas?" Boaz took the garments to the back of the stall and packed them away carefully.

Over the next three days word must have got out that their stall had some excellent wares, as they were kept very busy with customers. In fact they were able to sell all of their garments, except for the consignment for Kostas. This meant that

at the end of the third day they were able to have a big discussion with Jason regarding delivery tactics. Jason gave them
some detailed advice, with the main focus on safety and pro-
tection for them all. He assured them of his full support and
he promised them that he would go with them to deliver the
garments to Kostas at the villa right by the fort.

They packed up all their belongings and left them and their
donkeys at Jason's friends house, but kept two donkeys so
that Caleb could ride his own donkey, and the other one to
carry the load of garments for Kostas. They waited with Jason early on the fourth morning, at his stall, where he was still
selling potions to customers. Although he too had done well.
His stocks were low and he had had to send out for special
herbs to meet several customers' requirements. Now he had
gathered most of his belongings together, and had the barest
minimum on his stall. Suddenly a small boy ran up to them,
"Good sir, are you Caleb the Cripple? My master has sent me
to find you and lead you to meet him. He is looking forward
to receiving the garments for his lady." "Yes, that's me, we are
ready to come and meet with him. Jason, are you able to join
us?" "Coming, just give me a second to pack up my bits and
pieces here, I'll be right with you." He busied himself gathering
up his equipment, packing it into a small basket, which he then
loaded onto the pack donkey. Caleb picked up his staff, Joshua
brought him his donkey, he mounted and the little procession
followed the small boy through the narrow streets. They had
to struggle to keep up with him, due to the jostling crowds all
travelling through the streets, many of them on their way to
the temple, others searching for wares. Others were delivery
boys carrying bundles of varying descriptions to get goods
transferred from one place to another.

They passed through the gate and out towards the Roman fort situated just outside the walls. Here the crowds had more space to spread out, and there was room for them to walk together without losing each other in the throng. Eventually they came to the walls of a large villa. The boy led them in to a large courtyard where they tied up the donkeys. The boy ran off and returned quickly with a servant girl. "Hello, my name is Morgiana, let me show you the way to meet my master and his lady. Where are the garments?" "Right here in these packs, madam." Boaz indicated the packs on the back of the donkey. "Oh, that is more than I was expecting, hold on and I will get someone to give us a hand." She disappeared for a while, and eventually came back with two young men whom she directed to carry the packs. "Right, come this way. Kostas is here and expecting you." Caleb grabbed his staff, "Joshua, you stay here with the donkeys, and we will be back shortly." "I'll stay here with him, we'll keep our eyes and ears open and will be waiting for you;" said Jason, as he sat down on the low wall in the courtyard. He smiled at Joshua and gave the others a meaningful look. "OK, very well, you two follow me," and Morgiana set off, followed by Caleb and Boaz and the two servants carrying the packs containing the garments.

They passed through another small courtyard, down a colonnade lined with pillars, through another doorway and into a large atrium. Here there was a large table with several people seated on the lounges, drinking from goblets and eating various fruits. They were helping themselves from platters being passed around the company by exotic looking servant girls. Kostas was there with his wife, and on seeing them he got up and came towards them "Ah, Caleb, my good man, I see you have my garment assignment for me. My guests here havebeen waiting for your arrival with great anticipation! Good to see you made it to the villa without any difficulty. Priscilla, I think these folk have something for you!" He waved his hand in the direction of Caleb and Boaz. Morgiana came towards him, "My lady would like to try on the garments she was looking at previously, sir." "Ha," laughed Kostas, "I knew your curiosity would get the better of you Priscilla. So which ones did she see?" He asked Caleb, who moved over to the packs of garments; which had been placed on a bench by the atrium wall. He opened the nearest pack and extracted three tunics, which he handed to Kostas. "Nice, Caleb, very nice, I see why she picked these ones out. Here Morgiana, take these to Priscilla, so she can go and try them on." He said privately to Caleb, "Priscilla saw the cloak that you gave me for my wife, and has been on at me ever since to get something made by you, for her!"

Priscilla exclaimed "Well that's wonderful! Something to distract us from all that's going on in this place! Morgiana, bring those garments to my chamber. Come on ladies, let's see what these look like!" She left the atrium with two of her lady friends in close attendance. Kostas took Caleb and Boaz aside, "Right my good men, let's see what we have." He began to examine the garments and picked out a cloak of purple hue. "My goodness, Caleb, are you weaving for royalty now? This is magnificent! Well done, you have not let me down. I see that these are of high quality, and will fetch me some good prices in Tyre. So here, let me give you what is owing to you." He reached into his tunic, and brought out a leather pouch. He then counted out eighty silver coins. "Here my good men, this is what I owe you, two silver coins per garment, and ten extra for delivery on time. You will find that I have a hard reputation, but if you deal fairly with me, then you can be assured that I will be absolutely fair with you. You have done well. It is a pleasure doing business with you. I look forward to our ongoing business partnership. Now I will need another consignment of garments in about a years time, can you do a repeat order?" "Yes, absolutely sir. Thank you for your endorsement of our work. It has been wonderful to be able to provide this service for you. We will definitely be able to provide the next consignment by next year." "Good." He handed Caleb the pouch of money, "Then I will see you here in Jerusalem for next year's festival! Many thanks for your excellent work. Safe travels. Good bye, until we meet again." He waved his hand and then returned to his guests at the table.

One of the servant boys led the two men back out of the atrium to take them back to the outer courtyard. Caleb and Boaz were amazed at the amount of money they had received. Caleb had never held so much money in his hand at once. Whilst they were going down the colonnade Caleb silently passed the money pouch to Boaz, who tucked it safely away in his tunic. They got back to the courtyard, and Jason and Joshua stood up, unhitched their donkeys, helped Caleb to mount, and off they went back to the streets of Jerusalem. This time they were headed straight for Jason's friends house. It was mid-day by this time, and the crowds were even thicker than before. They made their way through the narrow streets and passed a covered section, where suddenly there were shouts and they heard the running of feet. Several zealots ran past them, hotly pursued by a group of Roman soldiers, led by the Roman Centurion Brutus. The soldiers all had their swords drawn and were intent on disposing of the troublemakers. Ordinary folk were doing their best to get out of the way and were pushing and shoving each other in their haste. Caleb's donkey got frightened and kicked out nearly unseating Caleb. The donkey's hoof connected with a soldier's knee, and the soldier yelled out in pain. Brutus reacted swiftly with his gladius sword slicing through the air and slashing Caleb across his torso. Caleb crumpled and fell from his mount. Jason observing all that was going on; suddenly took off his cloak and thrust it at Joshua, at the same time pushing him into an alcove. He leapt up onto a parapet and launched himself at Brutus, his foot connecting with Brutus's jaw. There was a loud crack as his neck broke and he fell to the ground, but Jason was still in motion. He picked up the fallen sword and thrust it at the next soldier, and did a flying leap catching the next two on their chins, knocking them both off their feet. He followed through with two more sword thrusts and turned to the last soldier, who was running his sword through one of the zealots. The next thing he knew was a blade slicing through his belly. It all happened so fast. The soldiers had never seen anything like it, and the people in the crowd just melted away. Jason glanced at Caleb, but saw that his eyes were already glazing over, there was nothing that anyone could do for him. He grabbed the donkey, and went back to Joshua, "Here, lad, give me back my cloak, hold the donkey and follow me." Boaz was in shock, "What just happened?" "Boaz, I'm sorry to say that Caleb is not with us anymore, but before anymore soldiers get here we have to move. They will want to know what has happened to their colleagues. Follow me." He led the two of them off up the street, and then ducked down a side alley, to get them away from the scene as fast as possible. They bumped into a man, who wanted to buy the black donkey, and offered two silver coins. So Jason took charge, as the others were too stunned to make any decisions. "Done, you can have him for two silver coins." They moved more quickly with only one donkey in tow, and soon reached the courtyard of his friend. Jason led them into the yard and called out to a boy to go and get his master. "Boaz, we have to leave now. We are wanted men. The soldiers will want revenge, so we have to move rapidly. Joshua do you have the money belt we prepared?" "Yes, here" He patted his side where a slight bulge could be seen under his tunic. "Good, you did as I advised. Right Boaz, both of you sit down for a second. What just happened is awful, I am so sorry for the loss of your father and friend. I too have lost a friend, and it grieves me that we could not do more for him. But now, we have to get away and find our way back to the safety of your homes and loved ones. Your families are dependant on you to get home and take up your lives, and continue to provide through your business for them." Joshua was still wide eyed, "My Papa, where is he? What's going on?" "Joshua, we have to leave now. There was nothing anyone or I could have done for your father. I am sorry to say he was killed, but it was sudden and quick. There is no way we could go back for his body, without jeopardising our own safety. So now he would want us to get back home safely, to look after our families." Jason explained gently but firmly. Boaz said, "But how did you do that? I have never seen anyone move like you did!" "I learnt some of those moves from a Chinese man I met on my travels, whilst I was learning my healing trade. Now no more discussion, ah here is Marcus. Marcus these are my friends, and sadly one of us has met with a Roman sword. So now I have some favours to ask of you. We need to get out of here quickly. Please can you buy my camels from me? We can use the three donkeys to leave here and head east for a bit, which is not where we would be expected to go, and then we can take the long route back to their village."

He took Marcus's arm and led him aside, "My friend, I am sorry to say that my good friend Caleb was murdered back there by the Roman soldiers. We have to leave here and I was wondering if you could supply some of your 'alternative' clothing?" Marcus looked shrewdly at his friend, "Jason, we have been friends for years! Look I can do better than just buy your camels. I have three horses in my stables, let us gather our things quickly. Give me a few moments, I will get my boy here to help me, and we will head over to my farm." He disappeared into the villa, leaving the three travellers standing there in the courtyard. Joshua was still reeling from the speed of events, and images of his father falling from his donkey still forefront in his mind. Boaz put his arm around Joshua's shoulders. "Alright my lad, we will go back home a different way. We will go back with Uncle Jason here, and he will guide us safely home." His tone was soothing and gentle, belying the turmoil within his own heart. Now that Caleb was gone, so many questions were flooding his mind.

After a short while, which seemed like ages, Marcus returned with some desert tribal clothes. "Here, put these on, these will help to disguise you and assist you in your getaway, they will make you look like tribal members and give you the right to be riding horses. Come let's go over to my farm where the main stables are, and I will get you mounted on some good horses that will get you home safely. Get on your donkeys for now, and follow me." He called one of his boys to get his horse, and they all followed him out of the yard.

They hastily threaded their way through the crowds still out on the streets, heading out of the city. A group of mounted soldiers galloped past them on their way into the city, raising a dust cloud as they went. Marcus led his small group out of the gates and they headed down the hill towards the farmlands on the outskirts of Jerusalem. The ground was dry and dusty, and the sparse vegetation on the hills around looked dry as well. There were still many travellers on the roads at this hour, many still heading into the city, whilst others, having done their business, were heading away. The small cavalcade mingled in amongst the other travellers, as they wound their way down the valley. The crowds were thinning out the further they got away from the city. Jason was keeping an eye out to see if they were being followed, but, so far, nothing was troubling the crowds; other than the fine dust that got into everything. They travelled in silence; it was difficult to have a good conversation along the road, separated from each other by different people. So they were all lost in their own thoughts as they made their way to the farm, Marcus turned on his horse, to look back at them and pointed with his finger; "Over there, follow me, we will go down this track." He headed off down a narrow track that wound around the hillside, and soon the crowds had disappeared and they had hills surrounding them. As they trotted on they came to a large cart track, which they joined and followed round another hill, and saw nestled in the little valley, a group of three farms in close proximity to each other. "Follow me, my farm is on the right."

He led them into the farmyard, and dismounted from his horse. A boy came running up to Marcus, and took his horses' reins. "Hello lad," He smiled down at the boy, "Hold this chap for me, but get him a drink. Is Charlie here?" "Yes sir, over in that stall sir. Your mare is in there delivering her foal right now!" Marcus turned to his fellow travellers, "Wait here, I will be right back. I just have to see what is going on in that stable."

He disappeared into the stall indicated. Five minutes later he came out with another lad. "This is Charlie, he will find you the horses I mentioned. Godspeed on your journey, and I wish for you all to get safely home. Forgive me, but I must attend to my favourite mare. I am hoping she will produce another fine foal like she did last year, but she is not having such an easy time at present, I think there may be a leg stuck. So if you'll excuse me, I will go and assist. By the way, don't worry about the horses. They are yours now; I will keep the camels and donkeys in exchange. Jason, see you next time! Bless you all!" "Marcus, you have done wonders already, thank you so much for everything." They embraced, and Marcus strode off, intent on his brood mare.

The three travellers looked at each other. Boaz tried to make light of the situation: "Ha, we look like the desert nomads! We will make a fine trio on horseback!" He got a faint smile from Joshua, who was looking pale and strained. He was still struggling with the turn of events. "Joshua, have you ever ridden a horse?" "Never!" came the short reply. "Well, son, you will have to learn real quick, as we have no other way of getting out of here! We have to put as much distance as we can between us and Jerusalem for the moment." Boaz was about to say more, when Charlie appeared leading three Arab horses. "The master says these three are for you, I hope they serve you well. They come from good stock and are fleet of foot, and will travel well in the desert! This one is Jenny, this one is Solomon, and this one is Gem." He handed the reins of Jenny, a beautiful palomino coloured horse, to Jason; and the reins of Solomon, a large grey horse to Boaz. "This is Gem, she is very sweet natured and gentle, she should do you well, take care of her." He handed the reins over to Joshua. The mare blew gently through her nostrils at him, and nudged him with her nose. "Well, girl, I hope we manage to get on all right." He hugged her, and then got up on her back. He watched as the other two got up on their mounts, having adjusted their packs, transferring what they needed from the donkeys. "Come on," said Jason, "Let's be off! Thank you Charlie, and again, please give your master my thanks. His help has been much appreciated. I hope the mare produces a great foal for him." Charlie waved them off, as they headed east to make their long way home!

CHAPTER 11

"Amazing things happen when you distance yourself from negativity."

Unknown

Throughout the long journey home, Joshua had been pondering all the events that had happened since he left home just a couple of weeks ago. Now as he neared their village, he experienced a huge sadness overwhelming him. There would be no father to welcome him, or help guide him through his teenage years. His mother would have to learn to cope without her beloved husband. His sister would have to look up to him as a big brother, as now she had no father to support her. The weight of the responsibilities felt heavy on his shoulders.

"Uncle Boaz, how are we going to cope without Papa? How are we going to get all the animals to be looked after properly, and how are we going to be able to do all the weaving that needs to get done?"

"Oh, Joshua, I have been thinking all about that myself. We will just have to do the best we can, and try and fulfil all the commitments that your father had between us. We will need to talk it all through with your mother and the other men working with us. Don't worry we will get it sorted out. Let's just be thankful that we are nearly home now, and we can tell everyone what has happened."

Jason added his thoughts, "Joshua, you are now very much part of the team that your father had in place. You are very fortunate that you have so many people around you, all working together. You will have to be able to step up and play your part as best you can. Your father will need you to be the best you can be." "That's right my boy, you have a great example to follow! Your Papa was an exceptional man."

They approached their village and soon they were spotted by Abigail and Naomi, who were out at the well drawing water for their families, "Hi, is that really you? How was your journey? We have been looking out for you! Where's Caleb? How come you're riding horses?" The questions tumbled out from Abigail, as she approached the trio. Boaz started to explain, but Jason chipped in: "There are a lot of things to tell, we best wait until everyone is together. Joshua, which one is your house? Let's go and find your mother." Aside, he said to Boaz; "Let us give the news to Zillah first, she needs to know from you and Joshua what happened, before everyone else finds out."

The three riders approached Joshua's house, and all three of them dismounted. Joshua started towards the house, and then hesitated. He looked to Jason and Boaz, "How am I going to tell her? Please come with me, it's too hard on my own. I don't know what to say!" "It's alright lad, we're right here with you, come on, let's find your mother." Boaz spoke with a gentleness and assurance he was far from feeling.

The three entered the house and saw Zillah, with Johanna in a cradle by her side, busy at the loom. Zillah stood up as they came in, "Hello? Oh Hello" she exclaimed, "I didn't recognise you in those strange clothes! My boy, so good to see you!" She hugged Joshua, who promptly burst into tears, and blurted out: "Oh, Mama, it has been awful, Papa got murdered by the Romans in the streets of Jerusalem, that's why we took so long to come home." He clung to his mother and sobbed and sobbed. Zillah looked over his head at the other two, with questions on her face! Then her eyes filled with tears as she began to absorb what Joshua was saying. "No," she cried in anguish, "My Caleb, oh, Caleb, what has happened?" She sank down onto a nearby chair, and pulled Joshua to sit down beside her. The door was flung open and Miriam rushed in, "Boaz, Boaz! You're home, we've been so worried for you all!" She flung herself at her husband, and he caught her up in a huge bear hug. He held her lovingly and firmly, but didn't say a thing. Miriam gradually realised the tension in the air, and looked up at Boaz, "What's happened?" she asked softly. "My love, Caleb was murdered in the streets of Jerusalem. Zillah is just finding out. She will need lots of support for these next few days, whilst she adjusts to this shattering news. We must all pull together and stay strong for each other." He held her close, so grateful that he was able to have his family together, so sorry for Zillah, Joshua and Johanna.

Jason was pleased to see that Joshua was finally able to cry and release his grief, safe in his mother's arms, but he was worried about Zillah, who was holding on to Joshua and just rocking him in her arms. Little Johanna began to cry, aware of the atmosphere within the room. Miriam realised this and knelt down and scooped up Johanna into her arms, "Come here little one, Aunty Miriam can give you a big hug. It's so good to have Joshua and Uncle Boaz home again. I am so sorry about your Papa." She hugged the baby girl close to her.

Jason went out to see to the horses and met Adam coming over to see what was going on. "Hello Adam, so good to see you. I have heard such good things about you! But I am sorry to have to pass on the sad news that Caleb was murdered in the streets of Jerusalem, and that is why we took so long to come back. Boaz is in there with Miriam and Zillah. I have just popped out to see to the horses, as we only got back about half an hour ago."

"Is it you Jason? How come you're here? What is going on? Caleb murdered? What happened? Sorry to ask so many questions, but it is all a bit sudden." Adam looked at Jason quizzically, thoughts whizzing through his mind as he began to assess the situation. Jason regarded Adam with an appraising look and was thrilled to see that he was a handsome man, who was now strong and fit, with a sense of purpose and direction to his life: having seen him a few years ago, when he had been a thin gangly young man, with little purpose, and no idea what he was going to do with his life. "My goodness, Adam, if I hadn't heard so much about you, I might not have recognised you. These last couple of weeks I have spent a lot of time with Caleb, Boaz and Joshua. We have become very good friends.

Now I find myself in the difficult situation of bearing bad news, I think it would be a great idea if you can call your shepherds here for a meeting, so that Boaz can discuss things with you all. Show me where I can put these dear horses out to pasture, they will need food and water. They have done us well, and carried us through all the difficult terrain on the east side of the country, as we headed back home to this village! There will be a lot to do over the next few weeks and months, as you will all have to adjust to the changes ahead."

Adam showed Jason where to take the horses, and helped him unload the panniers they had been carrying. "You can come and stay with Rebecca and myself if you like, my mother in law died recently, and we have a spare room available. You will need to rest and gather your thoughts after all the recent events. Thank you for all you have done for the guys. We are all very close, one big family. It is a huge shock to hear of Caleb's news. I am so sorry for Zillah and the children. We will all have to work even harder to make this work. Rebecca and I are so grateful to Boaz and Caleb for all that we have now: is because we were invited in to the family group. Life has really been so much better; before this most recent news. But I know we can pull through together."

Boaz came outside, and joined them, and helped carry the panniers towards the house. "Ah, thank you Jason for all you have done, we couldn't have gotten here without your help. What will you do for the next few days? Can you stay around for a bit, until we sort ourselves out?"

"Yes, my friend, I will not up and leave you just yet. Adam, here, has invited me to stay with him and his good wife, which will be perfect. I can catch up with them and be here to continue to be of assistance for at least another week or two. You just let me know how I can help, I am most certainly here for you. In the meantime I will look around for some herbs and plants I can use to build up my stocks again, and start to get back on the road when the time is right."

"My dear friend, you have been such a blessing to us all. Please stay and be our most honoured guest for as long as it takes. Go with Adam now, meet Rebecca and I will get us an evening meal sorted out. We can then all sit round the table and discuss what our next steps will be. See you then. Thanks Adam for your help too, you must both join us for the evening meal as well; see you later." Boaz then went back to the house to see what else could be done, and to find Miriam.

He entered the small house to find Zillah saying sadly: "He didn't stand a chance! My poor Caleb, having worked so hard, and then able to have safely delivered our large consignment to Kostas: for this to happen now is awful! My son, I am so sorry you had to witness this happen, but now, what are we to do?"

Boaz replied: "Sorry to come in on your discussion, but I think we have lots to talk about over the next couple of days! You are so right, it was so sudden and so much was going on at the time! Then to see Jason's response was also absolutely incredible, that man can move! The soldiers never knew what hit them. Jason then encouraged us to move swiftly, to get out of the streets and to get cracking on our journey, so that we are now here, safely out of the way! Joshua has done very well. He has coped with the sudden loss of his father, and the difficult journey we had coming home. Plus learning to ride a horse! You are a brave lad, my boy! Your father would have been proud of you!" He smiled approvingly at Joshua, but at the mention of his father being proud of him, Joshua dissolved into tears again. "That's just it, I wanted him to be here so much, so that I can make him proud with all that I can do. But now it has all changed. How can I get his approval when he isn't here?"

"Joshua," Boaz replied, "you are your father's son, you have guts and drive to get things done. He would want you to carry on and be the man of the family now. You are fortunate indeed: that you have been taught by a master weaver. I know that you have skills and talent, as I have seen your work; your father has taught you well. You will indeed be an amazing support for your mother and sister, but you must also remember that we are one big family now. You will not be expected to carry all the responsibility by yourself. Obviously it will all take time, but I know that you will develop your skills day by day."

"Thank you Uncle Boaz, thank you for all you have done for our family. I will try to do my best. Yes, Mama, you and Papa have been so close. I will do what I can. I can't be my father, but I will work hard, to the best of my ability."

"My son, I love you so much. Here, have a hug. The last few weeks have been a huge learning curve for you! Get some rest now. Let's not put the pressure on too much! We can discuss other matters later. Go and cuddle Johanna a bit, tell her of some of your adventures: she has missed having you around so much!" Joshua took Johanna from Miriam and settled down to hold her and rock her to sleep.

Boaz and Miriam sat down to have some time together. Zillah wanted to know all about what happened in Jerusalem, so she could really get a grasp of the turn of events. They talked softly, so as not to upset Joshua anymore. Boaz explained all that had happened since they had left to go to Jerusalem.

CHAPTER 12

"I am grateful for all of my problems. After each one was overcome, I became stronger and more able to meet those that were still to come. I grew in all my difficulties."

James Penney

Over the next three years the family worked hard in continuing to build the family business. Joshua struggled with the loss of his father, and went through some months of depression: he had been angry at the world in general for allowing the events to happen, resulting in the fact that now he was fatherless. He had been moody and uncooperative at times, which had put a strain on family relationships. Nevertheless, he had worked hard at his weaving, as had his mother, and they had managed to send off some more garments to keep Kostas supplied. This in turn meant that their fame as master weavers continued to spread. Not only had their businesses grown, but the flocks and herds were continuing to multiply and produce some of the finest wool in the region. The local women who were now experienced at spinning the wool, were getting it really fine, so the more superior garments were getting better and better. They continued with the experimenting with dye and were creating new colours for the wool, which gave them a head start over other weavers who were restricted to the local home spun dyes.

One evening Zillah sat holding Joshua's hand, as he lay on his bed on the roof-top. He had been sick for a few days and was complaining of severe stomach pains. His baby sister, Johanna, now just over three, was sitting at the head of the bed wiping his brow. Joshua was lying on his bed on the flat roof of their house. He looked pale and thin. He had grown quite a bit over the last three years, but was tall and gangly, still needing to fill out and develop a bit more. A fine sheet of sweat covered his face and body, whilst a light, welcome breeze moved a lock of his hair.

Joshua moaned and lifted a feeble hand to pat his mother's. His voice, barely a whisper managed to say: "Mama, it hurts so. So sorry I can't do anything, I should have done more for you." At that moment his aunt Miriam came up onto the roof, "How is he? Boaz has been working flat out looking after all the flocks; thank goodness David and Adam are helping with the lambing season. The sheep and goats are doing well." She approached the bed and knelt by her sister, "Oh, my goodness, Zillah, poor Joshua, he doesn't look well at all. Shall I go and fetch Jason? He has just arrived on a visit! He only got here last night." "Oh, Yes Miriam, that would be wonderful, please could you get him to come and look at Joshua, perhaps he will know what we can do for him." Miriam ran off to go and find Jason.

Zillah stroked Joshua's hand, "My son, my son what has happened to you? Ever since you got back from Jerusalem you have been struggling with one thing and another. I understand it was a huge shock for you, as it was for all of us. But you have gone through huge mood swings, bouts of depression and it has been so difficult for us all. I know that you have tried, and I forgive you for all the things you've said. You know that I love you, and will always love you?" Joshua opened his eyes, and squeezed his mothers' hand. He tried to give her a smile, but it barely reached his mouth, for his eyes looked so sad. Johanna reached over her baby hand, "I love you too, Josh, my super big brother." A tear trickled out of the corner of his eye, as he smiled a small smile at Johanna. He whispered, "Love you both so much." It was a huge effort to get even those words out.

Jason came running up the stairs, and over to the bed. He knelt down and looked at them all. "Hello, what's going on here?" "Jason, thank goodness you've come. Poor Joshua has been sick all week, but now he is unable to eat or drink, and says that his tummy hurts so. Can you do something for him?"

Jason looked at Joshua, "Hey son, what's up? Let me look at your tongue, can you stick it out for me? Ah ha, a bit dry. And let me look at your eyes, mmm, and now may I feel your tummy?" He placed his hands on Joshua's abdomen and began to feel gently. Joshua grimaced and winced as Jason's gentle probing hurt so much.

Jason noted a lot of things but didn't say any more. He took a deep breath, and sat back on his haunches. "Well, you are a pretty sick boy. The best thing we can do for you now, is to keep you as comfortable as possible. I will get a potion for some pain relief; we will give you some small amounts to start with. Bless you my son." He patted Joshuas' hand gently, and stood up. He looked at Zillah with sorrow on his face. "I'll be back later with some potion." Zillah looked at him, with red-rimmed eyes, as she had been weeping earlier, "Thank you for your help, it is a comfort to know that you are here at this moment." Jason nodded and left to go and collect the medicine, he knew that there was not much he could do.

Zillah gently brushed the lock of hair off his face, and bent and kissed him on the cheek. "Love you son," she said softly, as her eyes filled with tears again. "Shall I get him some water Mama?" Little Johanna so wanted her brother up and teasing her again. "Yes, darling, that would be lovely, be careful how you go." Johanna left to go downstairs to fetch the water from the water jar.

Joshua looked at his mother again, tried to say something, but then relapsed into a coma. His breathing was very shallow and the sheen of sweat on his face glistened in the sunlight. The shadows from the trees nearby played across his face. Johanna came panting up the stairs with the effort of being careful, and not spilling the water. "Here you are Mummy, can you give him some? Oh look he has gone to sleep!" Just then, Joshua gave a huge sigh, and stopped breathing.

Zillah watched closely, willing the next breath to come, but it didn't. She waited a minute, and then let out an anguished cry, throwing herself across his chest, she scooped her son into her arms, "Joshua, Joshua, not you as well! O my darling boy, what are we to do now?" She sobbed and sobbed.

Miriam came up to see how things were going, and grasped the situation in one glance, "Come here poppet, come and let Aunty give you a big hug." Johanna ran to her Aunt as they then consoled each other with a huge hug. Miriam's eyes were wet with tears, as she wept for her sister and her niece, grieving with them in her own sorrow, for Joshua was special to them all.

Jason came up the stairs carrying the potion, and saw it was too late. He bent over Joshua, and checked his pulse to confirm his suspicions, noted the pallor of the skin and that there he had stopped breathing. There was no pulse. He looked at the grieving women, and left them, to inform Boaz.

Poor Boaz would have to organize the funeral as soon as possible, as it was customary to bury the dead within twenty-four hours of death. There was a lot to organize, but there would be little help from either Zillah or Miriam at this moment. He ran down the stairs and out to the street.

CHAPTER 13

"Things often get tougher before they get easier. Stay strong, be positive. We all struggle sometimes. Your struggle is part of your story."

Unknown

Boaz had been busy since hearing the news of Joshua's death from Jason. He had been to the priest, who had arranged for the funeral to take place in the morning. They had the body embalmed that evening, so it would be ready for burial the following morning. Zillah and Johanna sat all night at the bedside, with Miriam keeping a vigil for Joshua.

The next day the whole town had gathered to grieve with Zillah. They all gathered in a large crowd behind the coffin, as it was being carried out to the burial grounds outside the town walls. Zillah, Miriam, and little Johanna were following the coffin closely, stumbling along in their grief and sorrow, followed by the mourners who were weeping and wailing loudly. The whole township was shocked at the sudden loss of this young man, whose father had been such an instrumental influence in bringing change to their whole community.

It had been Caleb that had introduced the members of the township to the dyeing procedures, and had encouraged many of the women to take up spinning as a full time occupation. The whole town had benefitted from his vision of growth and productivity. Now the heir to all that he had created had lost his life to disease, what was to become to all of them? Would they be able to carry on? Was Boaz the right person to take on the reins? So many questions were being raised. Not least of which was what was to happen to Zillah now that her main supports had been taken away? Boaz had his own cares to consider, as his family was still young and they had so many children to bring up themselves.

As they approached the town gates there was a noise of another large crowd processing towards them, being led by a travelling teacher. As the two bodies of people approached each other, they both slowed to a stop. The Teacher came up to the coffin, and a hush fell on everyone. He had such a presence about him, an air of authority and calm. He looked into the coffin, and told the bearers to put it down on the ground. They obeyed, and gently placed the coffin on the ground. The Teacher then went over to Zillah, and looked with such compassion into her face, "Woman, don't cry." He said to her, so gently and with such a depth of love, Zillah wept all the more! He then bent over the coffin and said; "Son, stand up!" Joshua stood up, and the crowds all gasped. "Come here son, step out of the coffin. Now woman, here is your son. Son here is your mother."

Zillah could hardly believe her eyes, as she clasped her son in her arms, "Oh, Joshua, is it really you? You are alive again! Lord have mercy on me, how can this be?" Johanna came running up and flung her arms around Joshua's knees, nearly making him fall to the ground, "Joshua, you came back!" she hugged his knees even harder, and Joshua had to steady himself on his mother. "Hey, little one, let me have my legs back!" The whole crowd of mourners had stopped crying, and were now shouting out with joy and thanksgiving; "He's come back from the dead!" Zillah reached up and kissed her son on his cheek, "Come on son, let's go home, you must be hungry? You look so well!" She looked around for the Teacher, to thank him. He was nowhere to be seen. The crowd he had been with had all gone, and those around her were her friends and members of the town. People kept coming up to Joshua to feel him, and to verify with their own eyes that here he was, very much alive! Someone ran up with a cloak for Joshua, as he struggled to get out of the embalming wraps. He freed himself and covered himself with the cloak, and they headed in a small procession, back to their house. Rejoicing all the way!

The whole family crowded into their small house, with many overspilling out into the street. They all wanted to hear what happened, and what he was going to say. "Settle down every-one, let's have some attention please. It's not everyday that someone gets raised from the dead! We all want to hear his story, so give him a few moments. Let him gather his thoughts and then let us all hear what he has to say!

Boaz encouraged him, "Come on Joshua, what happened, what's it like to be alive?"

"Yes," said Jason, "tell us of your experience, and what you remember!"

Joshua had been given a fresh tunic, and had got himself dressed properly again, and stood there, holding a scroll in his hand. Joshua suddenly realised that he was holding the scroll, and so slowly he opened and read it. Then with increasing amazement on his face, he pondered all the morning's events. Then he began to speak in a voice that was both strong, yet filled with wonder:

"You ask me what was it like? I wonder if you know what you are asking? I was caught up into a place filled with a very bright light. It was warm, and there was music, beautiful music like I had never heard before, playing and filling the atmosphere. I couldn't see where it was coming from, but it sounded like Heavenly music. I just knew in my heart that I had to be in Heaven! A man, dressed in a dazzling white robe, came up to me and started talking to me about my life. He was very kind and gentle, yet with a kingly aura about him. He noted that I had worked hard to please my parents, but then after Papa was killed I had become angry and bitter, and had let hate seep into my heart. The man was very understanding, and loving, he did not blame or accuse me. He offered me the opportunity to come back and help you, Mama, and to help Johanna grow up into a fine young lady! When I said Yes, I wanted to come back and support my family. He said, 'Good, now you have a mission to fulfil.' He told me that I was to help others to find the meaning of Life, and to live Life to the full, as an example to others. I am to help people to realise that we are here on this earth to love one another; to be kind and good; and to promote healing and wholeness to all those we meet.

I want to follow in my father's footsteps, and to help provide and care for my family. I also need to take up my inheritance left to me by my father, and to create an inheritance to leave to my children. I need to learn how to create more business for my family and for others in the community. I pledge to deepen my relationship with Kostas, as he has been such a support to us, even after the death of my Papa, he has stood by us and encouraged us. I have a lot to do!

The man then handed me a scroll. This scroll, and this is what it says:

KEYS TO LIFE

LOVE YOUR GOD - WITH ALL YOUR HEART.
Make Love your highest goal.
Persist until you succeed – never give up.
Be your self – you are unique.
Give back – bless others
Be honest – always act with integrity
Forgive – don't hold onto bitterness or anger.
Act now – make every day count.
Cultivate laughter – never go to bed angry
Leave a legacy.

So now I have work to do! I want to fulfil my destiny and to help and support my family. I pledge to keep up all that my father undertook, and to do as much as I can to support the community. I know that I have a lot to learn, but I will do all that it takes to become an even better weaver than my father was. We are fortunate to have such a strong and loving community. Let's all continue to grow together, supporting each other to the best of our abilities!

I know that we have a quota to fill for the next consignment to deliver to Kostas; so we had all better get cracking!" Joshua smiled a huge smile in the direction of his mother, and she in turn looked so proud of her son. He was truly stepping up, taking his father's place!

The whole room and all those outside clapped, and were thrilled with his new found air of authority and determination. They realised that Joshua was ready to step into his father's shoes, which meant that they would all continue to have work. Joshua looked around at everyone, "I have a commission to grow and develop our business with you all, so that in turn I can leave a legacy for my family as well as yours! Come on let's see this happen." He strode over to the loom.

Peace settled over the community and they all dispersed back to their homes. It was a wonderful day to be alive!

Keys to Life

→→ LOVE YOUR GOD - WITH ALL YOUR HEART.

→→ Make Love your highest goal.

→→ Persist until you succeed   never give up.

→→ Be your self   you are unique.

→→ Give back   bless others

→→ Be honest   always act with integrity

→→ Forgive - don't hold onto bitterness or anger

→→ Act now - make everyday count.

→→ Cultivate laughter - never go to bed angry.

→→ Leave a legacy.

This whole story is based on the scripture:

Luke 7 : 11 - 15

ABOUT THE AUTHOR

Fran Nguyen has worked as a Registered Nurse in England, Pakistan, and Australia, as well as in the Vietnamese Refugee Camps in Hong Kong. Whilst in Hong Kong, she worked with Y.W.A.M. in the camps and also with St. Stephen's Society, helping heroin addicts to recover. This was both with Chinese and Vietnamese people. With the help of Jackie, she set up a separate house for the Vietnamese people, which was then carried on by Gail Cogswell after she moved to Australia. She has also worked as a Counsellor, and a Case Manager for Transformations Drug Rehabilitation House in Brisbane, and a Youth Coordinator for Vietnam Grace Church in Brisbane.

Fran is a daughter, mother, grandmother, ex- wife, sister, aunt, friend and confidant, who has travelled to over 40 countries around the world. Fran found her WHY through being a missionary, reaching out and helping wherever God indicated. She is now an inpirational speaker and an author. She intends to gain support in order to go back onto the mission field within the next couple of years. You can contact her on globalimpactors88@gmail.com

Made in the USA
Lexington, KY
02 May 2018